THE FLIP SIDE
OF
HISTORY

THE FLIP SIDE

·········· OF ··········

HISTORY

STRANGE NEWS, HARD-TO-BELIEVE HEADLINES, AND OTHER CURIOUS STORIES FROM HISTORY

STEVE SILVERMAN

mango
PUBLISHING

CORAL GABLES

For permission requests, please contact the publisher at:
Mango Publishing Group
2850 S Douglas Road, 2nd Floor
Coral Gables, FL 33134 USA
info@mango.bz

For special orders, quantity sales, course adoptions and corporate sales, please email the publisher at sales@mango.bz. For trade and wholesale sales, please contact Ingram Publisher Services at customer.service@ingramcontent.com or +1.800.509.4887.

The Flip Side of History: Strange News, Hard-to-Believe Headlines, and Other Curious Stories from History

Library of Congress Cataloging-in-Publication number: 2020933909
ISBN: (p) 978-1-64250-220-6 (e) 978-1-64250-221-3
BISAC category code HUM016000—HUMOR / Form / Trivia

Printed in the United States of America

TABLE OF CONTENTS

One of my favorite true crime stories of all time. It's a case in which no one was talking but the green parrot.

A sad, yet unusual, human interest story that caught the attention of newspaper readers all across the United States.

Just what happens when person A attempts to kill person B, who unknowingly gets person C to kill person D instead?

A woman in a nightgown was seen clinging to the front of an automobile as it was being driven down the road. If your first thought was that the woman's life was in great danger and that the car should have been stopped, well, you would be wrong.

The unusual story of two high-flying aviators who attempted to pull off the perfect crime.

Every Christmas, there's that one popular toy that every child must have. Always in short supply, such a gift is so desired by children that parents are willing to pay top dollar to get their hands on one. This is the story of a popular Christmas gift that couldn't fit under the tree. If anything, this unusual gift was more likely to eat the tree.

Just what would make someone want to steal another person's shoes?

During the Great Depression, Le Mars, Iowa, was front-page news for three seemingly unrelated stories, all tied together by an incredibly misogynistic bequest made by one of its prominent attorneys.

Maybelle Knox was the center of perhaps the greatest mystery to ever occur in Le Mars. A story so fantastic, it captured the attention of an entire nation.

Perhaps the worst high school football team to have ever played was located around Salem, Massachusetts. There was a very good reason as to why they performed so poorly, and it had nothing to do with the quality of the team's players.

You've certainly heard about Mexican jumping beans, but have you ever witnessed jumping coal? Such a phenomenon was observed at a schoolhouse. At first, no one could explain why the coal was acting so strangely. Was it alive? Could the school have been haunted?

In 1954, Harold Jesse Berney, head of a Washington, DC, television antenna manufacturing operation, said he was chosen by the United States government to be its main contact with Uccelles, a prince visiting our planet from Venus.

The Concord Hotel in Kiamesha Lake, New York, was once the largest resort in the Catskill Mountains. Few people remember today, but it was once central to one of the most bizarre extortion schemes ever.

The amazing story of the only person in the United States to have been rescued from slavery four times.

Nothing on earth is permanent. As sure as there are forces that push mountains upward, there are opposing forces that will eventually bring them all back down. And no matter how hard humans may try, nature always wins in the end.

Nearly everyone wishes for a long, healthy, happy life. But a long life will most likely make you outlive everyone you know, which begs the question: is living a long life worth it?

PREFACE

During the winter of 1993, Principal Brian Howard of Chatham High School, the school where I spent my entire career as an educator, asked me to attend a seminar at the University of Albany on the teaching of authentic science research at the high school level. I never could have imagined how that one evening would change my life forever.

As presenter Daniel Wulff detailed how the program worked, he repeatedly referenced something that I'm quite certain the majority of the audience had never heard of: the internet, specifically email, which was necessary for students to keep in touch with researchers around the world.

It's difficult to describe how slow and clunky the internet was to use in 1993, particularly when accessing it from the rural setting of our school district. It required painfully slow dial-up modem connections over costly long-distance telephone lines that used text-based UNIX commands. As awful as this may all seem, it was cutting edge for its day, and I was immediately hooked.

Fast forward to the summer of 1994 and I read about a new invention called the World Wide Web. I fired off an email message to Steve Janover—instructional coordinator at the Northeastern Regional Information Center (NERIC), and my internet guru in those early days—questioning him about it. He told me that NERIC was testing the web out, but he wasn't sure if it would catch on. I drove up to see him and he demonstrated the World Wide Web to me.

Upon returning home, I immediately set to work on my first webpage: my resume. A few days later, I began to construct my first real website. I simply uploaded some interesting facts that I had shared with my close friend Jamie Keenan. This included how they placed the Ms onto M&Ms, the history of

Vaseline, and other similar stories. For lack of a better title, I remembered that one of my students, Steve Lotz, had told me that I knew more useless information than anyone else. So I typed the words "Useless Information" at the top of the page, and my website was born.

Initially, few people ever looked at what I wrote. However, everything changed over the 1997 Fourth of July holiday. Yahoo had chosen my website as their Pick of the Week, and it wasn't long before my page began receiving more than one million views per year—an astronomical number of visitors for that time period. From that website, two compendiums of my favorite stories were published in book form: *Einstein's Refrigerator* and *Lindbergh's Artificial Heart*.

With the advent of e-books, it was predicted that physical copies of books would ultimately become obsolete. As a result, I gave up on the idea of ever writing a third volume of stories and turned my attention toward a new technology: podcasting. On January 27, 2008, the *Useless Information Podcast* was born. I have been researching, writing, and recording new stories for the podcast ever since.

Yet as I write this, the prediction that print books would become just a memory has still not yet happened. When I was first approached by Natasha Vera, an editor at Mango Publishing, to write this book, my initial reaction was to turn the opportunity down. I knew from working on my first two volumes that writing a book such as this was a grueling, time-consuming process I wasn't sure I wanted to repeat. But after a couple months of discussing the idea with my wife and friends, I decided to take the plunge and write the book that you now have in your hands.

To me, writing a non-fiction book is a scary proposition because every word is permanent. Unlike the web or a podcast, no changes can be made to a book once it has been printed. While I have thoroughly researched each story, there are sure to be errors. Hopefully they are limited to minor things such as a misspelling or an incorrect unit conversion.

Researching long-forgotten and obscure stories can be frustratingly difficult, and questions always come up along the way. Inconsistencies in the source material were common, requiring me to make a judgement call as to what was indeed the correct fact. At other times, I was left with questions that I was unable to answer, such as when exactly someone was released from prison, or what happened after the story disappeared from the headlines. You may find yourself asking similar questions. Should you have any further information on a story, please do not hesitate to reach out and let me know.

A few comments about conversions: The vast majority of measurements contained within this book are approximations. While 5,000 miles does equal 8,046.72 kilometers, this figure would be rounded to 8,000 kilometers for easier reading. In addition, currency values have been adjusted to 2018 values, the most recent dataset available at the time of this writing.

I do hope that you enjoy the stories I have chosen to include. If there is any common theme that runs throughout this book, it is that each story has something a bit quirky to it. Some will make you happy, some will make you sad, and some may even make you mad—yet they are all totally true.

Enjoy!

STEVE SILVERMAN

JANUARY 2020

PART 1

RUN-INS
WITH THE LAW

The Green Parrot Murder

1942

One of my favorite true crime stories of all time. It's a case in which no one was talking but the green parrot.

Nestled between a dollar store and the Moon House Chinese-Japanese restaurant is an unassuming building located at 1806 Third Avenue in New York City's Harlem neighborhood. Today, it's just a drab, mustard-colored, five-story brick building with glass blocks at ground level that fill in what were once storefront windows. What few people know is that on Sunday, July 12, 1942, this building was the scene of an incredible murder story.

Back then, the lower floor of the building was home to the Green Parrot Bar & Grill. The restaurant was owned by a guy named Max Geller, and was named after its mascot—a large, foul-mouthed, green parrot. If you fed him a cracker, he would let loose a steady stream of expletives. That fateful Sunday in July, police received a report of a shooting at the bar. When they arrived, they found Geller lying on the floor at the base of his pet parrot's perch. There was a bullet wound that went right through his voice box, making it impossible for police to question him on what had happened. Within moments of the police's arrival, Geller fell into a coma.

This should have been an easy crime to solve. At the time of the shooting, there were more than twenty patrons in the bar. Police tried to interview each of the witnesses, but they were all reluctant to say anything. After all, this was Harlem—a part of the city notorious for crime, where no one spoke to the police. Detectives learned that, while there was one waiter on duty, Geller was alone behind the bar when a mysterious man entered the restaurant. And then... And then... Well, no one was sure. There were twenty witnesses and twenty different stories.

While those that sat in the dining room had good reason to claim not having seen anything, a number of people that were physically standing at the bar when the crime occurred still alleged that they had no clue what happened. A few of the eyewitnesses were certain the shooter walked in with his gun already drawn. Others said the gunman had pulled the weapon out of his pocket after approaching the bar. One person was sure it was a stickup and said they saw the gunman run behind the bar and empty the cash register of its contents.

1940 tax photograph of Geller's Green Parrot Bar & Grill.

Investigators broadened their search and questioned people that lived and worked in the surrounding neighborhood. Although a few people did see a man running down the street with a gun in his hand, none provided anything more than a vague description of the desperado.

All through the witnesses' questioning, that green parrot wouldn't keep his trap shut. The agitated bird kept blurting out phrases like "It's murder!" and "Robber! Robber!" in addition to several curse words.

This led Captain Mahoney, a detective with the city's police department, to state, "What a case! A dying man who can't talk, twenty witnesses who won't, and a squawking parrot we can't shut up."

I know what you're thinking. Maybe, just maybe, that squawking parrot was onto something. However, it was quickly revealed by regulars of the bar that the parrot's best trick was screaming "It's murder!" in a high-pitched voice and startling unfamiliar patrons from their seats.

Detectives also ruled out the robbery theory. A quick check of the cash register's receipts showed that about thirteen dollars were missing, but the rest of the cash was still in the till. They deduced that Geller had probably paid out the missing cash for a delivery earlier in the day.

When Geller died three weeks later on August 2, the shooting became a murder. Assistant District Attorney Louis B. Pagnucco was assigned to the case and requested that all of the witnesses be brought into the police station for further questioning by the detectives.

Once again, the questioning led nowhere. That is, until Pagnucco stepped out of his office for a breath of fresh air. It was then that he noticed two female witnesses engaged in a conversation. One of the women appeared agitated, and the two were speaking in a foreign tongue (at least one foreign to those like myself who only speak English). And yet, it wasn't foreign to Pagnucco. The DA was different from the average man in that he supposedly had the ability to fluently speak more than a dozen different languages. While the women were talking at a very low volume, he was able to deduce that they were speaking in Quebecois, a French dialect spoken only in Canada.

Pagnucco did the wise thing and didn't let on that he understood everything they were saying. He just listened with an attentive ear, pretending to not have a clue. The gist of their conversation was that they should tell the detectives they had no knowledge of what had transpired that night. Pagnucco learned that both women had fibbed and told their husbands they were going to see a movie. They were fearful of the repercussions should their husbands discover they had been at a bar. In particular, he heard one tell the other, "They wouldn't understand and you know what your husband will do to you if he finds out." Pagnucco interpreted this to mean that she would get the beating of a lifetime, and decided to use this detail to his advantage.

The questioning of the first woman started routinely: her name, address, and a few general questions about the crime. As planned, she said that they hadn't seen anything. That's when Pagnucco cornered her. "By the way," he questioned, "about your girlfriend: does her husband really beat her up?"

She didn't respond to his question in English, so he restated it in Quebecois. At that point, she realized he understood every word the two women had exchanged.

The witness then broke down crying and confirmed that the two women did get a quick glance of the killer. She said that they both heard Max Geller shout before the murderer pulled out a gun and fired.

The second woman was then interviewed and told the same exact story. Neither knew the gunman, but both commented that he looked familiar. All they could add was that he was dressed in an unforgettable black-and-white-checkered suit. However, the flashy suit lead went nowhere.

Pagnucco requested that a top-notch police detective named John J. Morrisey be assigned to the case. Morrisey immediately went to the scene of the crime and practically moved into the place. He tried teaching the green parrot his name, but realized it was not that easy. The bird could only learn a new phrase by repeating it over and over, ad nauseum.

"I've noticed that every time the parrot calls out the name of some customer, it usually decorates the name with the same group of oaths," Morrisey stated. "I made a note of some of them and checked with men who were first at the scene. They remembered that the parrot used some of these same phrases after yelling what sounded like 'robber.' "

The fact that the bird kept repeating the words "It's murder!" and "Robber! Robber!" shortly after the crime occurred puzzled him. Those that frequented the bar stated that they had never heard the bird say the word *robber* before. And since it took time to teach the bird any new words, it couldn't have picked up the term so easily during the time of the shooting.

To Pagnucco, Morrissey must have seemed crazed when he stated that he believed the bird was not saying "Robber! Robber!" Instead, he concluded that the bird was blurting out the name of someone with whom he was well acquainted, someone who had taken the time to repeatedly say his name to the bird until he mastered it, someone by the name of Robert— as in "Robert! Robert!" If the bird was saying his name over and over, could that Robert possibly be the murderer? It was an incredible long shot, but they had little else to go on.

Police canvassed the neighborhood and narrowed their focus down to two men named Robert, both of whom had mysteriously disappeared on the night of the crime.

One of the missing Roberts was Robert Schultz, a frequent customer of the Green Parrot. He had been living in a nearby rooming house before suddenly packing up his bags and leaving town. Police were initially unable to locate Schultz, but then received a call from his landlady that he had returned. Schultz was then picked up and brought in for questioning. He denied any knowledge of the crime. It was confirmed that he arrived at his father's farm in the Midwest the day after the crime occurred. The train ride took several days, which meant that he had to leave New York several days before Geller's murder. That robber—I mean Robert—was crossed off their short list of suspects.

That left just one Robert as a possible suspect, a guy named Robert Butler. Butler operated a taxi stand a few doors down from the Green Parrot and disappeared on the night of the murder. His wife stated that he had grown frustratingly tired of operating a cab at night and didn't come home one evening after work. She had not seen him since.

Butler's wife seemed to have no concern that her husband had suddenly disappeared without a trace. The detectives suspected that he was still secretly in contact with her and worked with the postal service to track all of the mail addressed to Mrs. Butler, but none of it matched her husband's handwriting.

One year after the murder occurred, police had still not located Robert Butler. Investigators were convinced that he was contacting his wife in some way, though they did not know how. The mail route was ruled out, and the couple did not have a phone.

Pagnucco suggested that the post office track the mail of Butler's best friend, in case he was receiving the messages and passing them on to Butler's wife. They received word that the friend had received a letter postmarked Baltimore, Maryland, but it lacked a return address. They needed to find out what was in that envelope, but if they opened it, Butler's friend would have realized that his mail was being watched.

Instead, DA Pagnucco hatched a plan. They arrested Butler's friend, claiming that he matched the description of a man suspected of assault and robbery. They brought the so-called suspect down to headquarters and told him that they were awaiting a positive ID from an eyewitness. In the meantime, they said they had to check all of his belongings to make sure he didn't have the stolen loot on him. This was all a bunch of hooey, but they needed a way to get a look at that letter.

It was at this time that one of the detectives took a pile of papers out of the suspect's pockets and spotted the letter with the Baltimore postmark in the stack. That detective quickly left the room to read the letter while another distracted Butler's friend. Upon returning, he slipped the letter back into the pile of papers and said he couldn't find anything.

After releasing the friend from custody, the detective who had read the letter confirmed that it was from a guy named Robert and contained information stating his whereabouts. He was working the midnight shift at Bethlehem Steel in Baltimore.

Off to Baltimore, Pagnucco and Morrisey went. They parked themselves right at the front gate of the plant. Hundreds of employees walked by the two men before they spotted Butler in the crowd.

As one would expect, Butler denied any involvement in Max Geller's death. He claimed to have gotten into a fight with his wife that night and left her.

While on the train back to New York City, Butler questioned why they suspected him. Pagnucco asked "What do you think of Geller's parrot?" to which Butler answered, "Smart bird."

The DA countered with "I'll say. He's the one that told us you did it." This was followed by a few more sentences before Butler jumped in and said, "I never did like that bird." He then confessed to the murder.

Butler said that on the morning of the murder, he had been part of a big dice game. A few of the players asked him for a loan but he refused, sensing that they would never return the money. These thugs, in turn, threatened Butler's life. He retreated to his home and grabbed his gun, just in case they really did come after him. In an effort to calm his nerves, Butler turned to a bottle of alcohol.

Later that day, Butler finally stepped outside and went to the Green Parrot Bar & Grill. Seeing that his friend was already drunk as a skunk, Geller refused to serve him another drink. That was when Butler pulled the gun and fired at him.

On February 10, 1944, Butler was sentenced to seven to fifteen years in Sing Sing.

Sues for Canary's Lost Love

1917

Mrs. Anna Mallott filed a lawsuit in a Syracuse, New York, court against her neighbor, Mrs. Martha Traylor, for the alienation of the affections of her pet canary, Pete. She sought $500 (nearly $10,000 today) in damages.

Mrs. Mallott said that the canary had escaped from her home after she left the door open. In an effort to locate her lost pet, she placed advertisements in local newspapers and offered a reward for his return.

She argued that Mrs. Traylor was able to coax the canary into a cage and had been in possession of the bird ever since. Mrs. Mallott claimed that the bird was hers, "…for she has often heard it singing and knows its voice, but that she has been unsuccessful" in getting Mrs. Traylor to return Pete.

Tender Young Alice, They Say

1949

A sad, yet unusual, human interest story that caught the attention of newspaper readers all across the United States.

On February 28, 1949, there was a new baby born into this world and her name was Alice. At six weeks of age, Alice would become national news.

Born in Houston, Texas, Alice lived with her dad, forty-five-year-old Clyde Emmitt Roco, at the Hou-Tex Grain company. Her home was incredibly unusual and made from 100 percent pure glass. In many ways, it was similar to a greenhouse, but significantly smaller. Specifically, Alice was being raised inside of a large glass bottle—an inverted 5-gallon (18.9 liter) water jug—similar to the plastic ones found atop water coolers today.

The thing is, Alice was, in fact, a feathered Dominique chicken. When she was a fuzzy baby, before anyone could determine if Alice was a he or a she, Roco made the decision to raise her inside of the bottle. Alice was placed on display inside the feed store, with a paper sign that read "Watch Me Grow" above her. As Alice grew larger, her weight was periodically recorded in the blank space on the sign.

Roco did make a few modifications to the bottle as Alice increased in size. First, small holes were drilled into it for increased air circulation. Once the glass home became a bit too constrictive for Alice to eat properly, he drilled a larger hole into its side. This allowed Alice to extend her head out through the opening and easily reach the two containers filled with fresh food and water.

Overall, Alice didn't appear to be suffering in the slightest. She ate heartily, grew into a plump 2¼-pound (approximately 1 kg) bird, and clucked as all hens do. The only thing Alice couldn't do was move around—she was confined to a glass prison cell.

Roco understood that not everyone would be happy with Alice's living arrangements. He knew that, at some point, someone would become upset with how she was being raised. And he was right. Six separate complaints were filed with the local chapter of the Society for the Prevention of Cruelty to Animals (SPCA).

W. S. Poe, an SPCA commissioned officer, was dispatched to Roco's feed store on April 13 to investigate. Upon his midafternoon arrival, Poe found exactly what had been described in the complaints: a chicken being raised in a glass water jug. Not long after he began his investigation, Poe stumbled over some potatoes and damaged them, and was thus forced to leave. He promised, "I'll be back later." Poe kept his word and upon his return, he tried to seize Alice and her glass enclosure, but employees at the store passed the bottle around in a "basketball fashion" to prevent him from taking possession. He left empty-handed.

Within twenty-four hours, the story was picked up by the United Press and shared with readers across the United States.

Mrs. C. E. Appleby, superintendent for the Houston SPCA, declared that confining Alice to the glass bottle was "sheer cruelty."

Roco vehemently denied that Alice was suffering in any way. "Some lady called me yesterday—wouldn't give her name—and said she heard this chicken's feet were so sore she couldn't stand up." He added, "If there's a chicken in this town with any more perfect feet, or any more perfect anything than Alice, I'll donate $1000 [approximately $10,650, adjusted for inflation] to the SPCA."

Roco's attitude simply enraged those at the SPCA, who were determined to free Alice from her glass jug. They threatened legal action against Roco if he did not let her out immediately.

But Roco refused. He told the press that placing Alice in the glass jar was an experiment designed to prove that a chicken could thrive on quality feed and a minimal amount of exercise. He stated, "Without all that running around that other chickens do, she'll really make good eating."

Mrs. Appleby was outraged and told the press, "This thing has gone beyond the experimental stage, and we'll take the chicken out of the bottle and hold it at the shelter until this is settled."

Roco did admit that his so-called experiment had been sponsored by an unnamed feed producer, and was done to generate publicity for both the store and the manufacturer.

The war of words between the two sides continued, and with the SPCA moving closer to filing charges against him, Roco was forced to hire an attorney.

Texas Civil Statute Article 761k, which was intended to protect poultry from cruelty, required that the birds be housed in "coops, crates or cages made of open slats or wire on at least three sides, and of such height, that the fowls can stand upright without touching the top, and shall have troughs or other receptacles with ease of access at all times by the birds confined therein." The law made no mention of allowing for glass jugs.

On Saturday, April 16, 1949, Roco made the decision to put an end to this entire controversy. He grabbed a hammer, smashed the glass jar, and fractured it into several pieces.

After six weeks of confinement, Alice was finally free and…

She just stood there and didn't move. After some time, Alice finally began to cautiously walk around the table on which her former home once stood.

G. A. Briscoe, a representative for the company that supplied Alice's feed, stated, "I've seen this thing done before." He added, "A chicken will stay still for a week or so, out of habit, you know, if it isn't moved."

It appeared as if the SPCA had won. Mrs. Appleby later commented, "I surely do consider it a big victory for the SPCA. I'm glad it's all over and was settled peaceably. Now I can get some sleep."

It would prove to be a shallow victory.

Shortly after Alice gained her freedom, Roco gave her to his attorney, W. Giles Roberts. He accepted her to cover his "fee." Roco stated, "Hey, she will make a good meal."

The next day, April 18, 1949, was not a good one for Alice, as her forty-ninth day of life also became her last. Mr. and Mrs. Roberts made Alice the centerpiece of their Easter Sunday dinner, later commenting that she made for "fine eating."

It is difficult to say which side won here—the SPCA for freeing Alice, or Clyde Roco for getting the last dig in. Either way, it is very clear that the only one who lost was Alice.

An Unusual Chicken Thief

1925

Police arrested William English, John Carner, and Thomas Simpson on July 1, 1925, for the theft of chickens from a coop located at the home of John D. Fell on Upper Lake Street in Elmira, New York.

Simpson was found sleeping in the back of Carner's car and told the judge that he had played no part in the theft of the chickens. He explained that he had simply hitched a ride from Ithaca to Elmira with Carner. The judge dropped the charges and Simpson was released.

Carner, however, was caught red-handed. In one hand he held apparel stolen from the Fell's clothesline, while his other held several chickens. He told the judge that the police had gotten it all wrong. He wasn't taking the chickens from the Fell yard. Instead, he said that he had been transporting the chickens from Ithaca when they escaped from his car. At the time of his arrest, he was in the process of placing those escaped chickens back into his automobile.

It was soon determined that fifty-six-year-old Carner was responsible for a number of chicken thefts around the region. While none of the thefts individually amounted to grand larceny, altogether they caused a great loss to the farmers.

Carner, who had previously served time in prison, pleaded guilty to the charges of burglary in the third degree, and petit larceny. He was sentenced to a five-year term at Auburn Prison. His co-conspirator, William English, pleaded guilty to a charge of burglary in the third degree. He was given a ninety-day sentence and ordered to pay a fine of $200 ($2,900 in today's money).

A Date with Death

1938

Just what happens when person A attempts to kill person B, who unknowingly gets person C to kill person D instead?

Dolores Myerly. That name probably means absolutely nothing to you. And there is a good reason for that: she was born in obscurity, she lived in obscurity, and if it weren't for one little sip of alcohol, she would have died in obscurity.

Little is recorded publicly about Myerly's life, but here is what I was able to piece together. First, Dolores Myerly was not her real name. She was born Marie Bayouth in Oklahoma on April 19, 1919, to Alex and Bessie Bayouth. She died a bit shy of her nineteenth birthday. Her body was identified by her sister, Mrs. Ted Myerly of Jacksonville, Florida, and then transported back to Tulsa for burial in the Rose Hill Memorial Park Cemetery. Just how and when Marie Bayouth transformed herself into Dolores Myerly is neither known, nor needed, to tell her story.

Perhaps the most important thing to note was that Myerly was supposedly a member of the world's oldest profession. She had been staying at the San Juan Hotel in Orlando, Florida, for the ten days prior to her death. On February 15, 1938, Myerly found herself in Jack Holloway's, a bar within a short walking distance of her room at the hotel. It was there that she met forty-one-year-old Robert Etty of nearby Pine Castle, and the two struck up a conversation.

A pudgy, balding painter by trade, Etty was making ends meet through a combination of legitimate work at the bar and dealing illegal card games in the rear of the establishment to supplement his income. Etty later said, "I'd never been with her before, but I'd heard several of the fellows talking about her. She asked me for $15 to pay her room rent, and I told her that I didn't have it but that I'd try to get it." He added, "She told me that I was just giving her the runaround, but I told her I'd see her about midnight, after I got off from work."

Dolores Myerly had just made a date with death.

Around 11:45 that evening, Etty made his way up to room 208 at the San Juan. He was greeted by Myerly, who was scantily clad in a thin silk slip, stockings, and shoes. As Myerly got closer to Etty, she could feel a miniature bottle of alcohol in his pocket. He offered her a drink, and she mixed the bottle's contents with water in a tumbler. Etty said, "Hey, don't drink it all, save some for me."

He then described what happened next. "She put the tumbler to her lips, took a sip, started to walk toward the bathroom and came back toward me, asking, 'What did you put in this?' "

Those were the last words that Dolores Myerly, a.k.a. Marie Bayouth, ever said. She suddenly dropped to the floor near the foot of her bed.

SAN JUAN HOTEL, ORLANDO, FLORIDA

"ORLANDO'S LARGEST AND FINEST"

Postcard of the San Juan Hotel dated "Not After 1941."

Etty panicked and immediately sought help. While awaiting assistance, he tried to comfort Myerly by applying wet towels to her head. Dr. Duncan McEwan, a resident of the hotel, was first on the scene, but was unable to revive her. He stated, "The girl died within five minutes after I arrived."

The fact that Myerly succumbed so quickly, coupled with the distinct almond smell observed on both the tumbler and bottle, brought the immediate suspicion of cyanide poisoning. That would later be confirmed by laboratory tests.

A search by police of Myerly's room turned up nothing out of the ordinary: a newly penned letter to her sister expressing how much she liked Orlando and its residents, a couple of newly purchased suitcases, a new pair of riding boots, some change in her pocketbook, eight one-dollar bills hidden inside a package of Kleenex tissues, several pawn tickets, and a number of love letters. On her dresser was a dog-eared copy of *Love Stories*. There was also the usual assortment of clothing and toiletries, but not a single shred of evidence suggested that she was unhappy or intended to take her own life.

This could mean only one thing: Etty murdered Myerly with that poisoned bottle of alcohol. But if he was the murderer, why did he seek help so quickly? Was he trying to cover his tracks by pretending to be concerned?

Etty was the one and only suspect in the case, but he offered up the most bizarre of excuses. He claimed that an unidentified man had given him the poisoned whisky about forty-five minutes prior to his meeting with Myerly. "He had the bottle in his hand at the time and I asked him what he was going to do with it. He tried to hand it to me saying, 'You take it, I don't drink whisky—I drink beer.' " Etty continued, "I offered to buy him a bottle of beer and we went into the taproom and he drank it. As he left, he stuck the bottle of whisky in my pocket." Etty added that the man said something about losing $125 in a poker game and described the unknown suspect as "wearing a small mustache, [weighing] about 130 pounds and [standing at about] 5 feet 7 inches tall."

Robert Etty was then placed under arrest as the police began their investigation. Accompanied by a detective, he was released from jail just long enough to search for the mysterious mustachioed man, if he truly did exist.

Their first stop was the tavern itself. Owner Jack Holloway confirmed that Etty had purchased a bottle of beer for someone who matched the mystery man's description. Yet, he was unable to confirm that this man had passed the tainted bottle of whisky to Etty. A porter at Holloway's was able to supply one piece of evidence critical to the search: he remembered that the suspect was having problems with his dentures.

A check with local dentists led them right to the suspect.

On February 17, police arrested Donald Long at his home at 627 East Washington Street in Orlando. The thirty-three-year-old, married, father of two fit Etty's description perfectly, excluding the fact that he was clean shaven. Under questioning, Long admitted that he had shaved his mustache off the previous evening.

Long wasn't exactly what one would call a model citizen. In 1931, he was sentenced to two years in the penitentiary for stealing a car. After his release in 1934, he somehow landed a job as a plainclothes officer for the Orlando Police Department. After public outcry over his appointment, he was transferred to the city's sanitation department to drive a truck. Long had also been questioned in the unsolved October 5, 1937, murder of a man named Frank Beane. Shortly after the murder took place, Long contacted Sheriff J. C. Stone, who later testified, "He called me on the telephone and asked me to come out and get the gun, which he claimed was hidden in his garage by an unidentified person. His exact words were: 'You come and get it. I'm afraid it might have been used in a murder.' " Sure enough, a gun of similar caliber to the one used in Beane's murder was found in Long's garage. But we'll get back to that later...

Upon being brought in for questioning on the death of Dolores Myerly, Long asked the officer to stop at a local drugstore so he could purchase two capsules of sodium amytal (the legal limit without a prescription at the time), which he downed with a bottle of beer. Needless to say, he was whacked out of his mind by the time he arrived at the police station. As he sobered up, Long admitted to everything except giving Etty the bottle of liquor and gambling away $125. He also denied ever meeting Dolores Myerly and stated, "Etty lies when he says I told him I didn't drink whisky and handed him the bottle! I do drink whisky and I didn't have that bottle of whisky on me!"

The next step in the investigation was tracking down the source of the cyanide. Druggist E. K. Enzor of nearby McElroy's Pharmacy told police that he had sold two boxes of cyanide to a chiropractor named Dr. Ernest N. Sykes the day before the murder occurred. When questioned, Sykes said that he had delivered the cyanide to Long, who had asked Sykes how much of it would be necessary to kill a man. Sykes replied, "About as much as you can get on the point of a knife."

All signs now pointed directly to Long, which meant that he had intended to poison Etty, but accidentally killed Dolores Myerly instead. But what was the motive? The two were barely acquainted, and neither seemed to have any dislike for the other.

Upon being called to the witness stand to testify at the coroner's inquest, however, Dr. Sykes proved that he wasn't exactly the most reliable of witnesses. He suddenly changed his story and claimed that he had purchased the cyanide for another man: George Coston.

Coston, a former captain of the Orlando Police Department, was recently defeated in the prior sheriff election. Since the loss, Coston had been running his own private detective agency. He was also a longtime patient of Sykes, who now claimed that Coston asked him to purchase the cyanide. Sykes stated, "The last batch I delivered to him the morning of the fatal night."

On February 19, Long, Sykes, and Coston were held on murder charges, while the man who killed Dolores Myerly, Robert Etty, was released. The pieces to the puzzle were starting to come together.

Remember the gun that was found in Long's garage? Long claimed that Coston had helped him avoid being charged in the murder of Frank Beane after the gun was found on his property. As repayment for his services, Coston insisted that Long join his detective agency. The business was actually a cover for a series of crimes that Coston had planned to commit. These included the assassinations of several men (one of whom was the sheriff that beat him in the election), the robberies of several jewelry stores, the theft of the contents of a Sears, Roebuck, and Co. safe, and the robbery of valuables from several prominent citizens.

The best part of Coston's scheme was that he never intended to do any of the dirty work himself. He was going to leave that up to Donald Long and Edward "Buck" Moseley, an eighteen-year-old who was serving a suspended sentence for robbery.

The biggest problem with the scheme was that Long never committed any of the crimes Coston had planned. Long stated, "Coston was beginning to get angry because I had not gone through with any of his planned robberies or murders. He was threatening me."

Death certificate for Marie Bayouth.

On the evening prior to Dolores Myerly's murder, Coston picked Long up and drove out to the Colonialtown neighborhood of Orlando to take care of some business. That was when Long told Coston that he was through. "Coston told me if I ever squealed, he'd blow my brains out and kick 'em all over Orange Ave." He added that Coston wanted to have a drink to end their partnership, but Long declined because he had been drinking beer and claimed to get sick if he mixed the two. Long continued, "He took a drink and killed the remains of a pint bottle. Then he reached in the back of his car and pulled out a miniature and gave it to me."

It should come as no surprise that Coston denied everything. "We never planned any robberies. We never planned any murders," he insisted. "I used Long on odd jobs around my private detective agency."

The real question was whether a jury would believe a bizarre story in which person A (Coston) intended to kill person B (Long) who, in turn, unintentionally had person C (Etty) unknowingly kill person D (Myerly).

At trial, Donald Long, Dr. Sykes, and several lesser witnesses all testified against Coston. Perhaps the most damaging evidence was a series of thirty-three notes that Coston penned while in the Orange County jail and had smuggled through an intermediary to Long. The notes told of Coston's nervousness while he sat in jail, and placed intense pressure on Long to get Buck Moseley out of town so he wouldn't squeal. Coston instructed Long to flush the notes as soon as he read them, but for some reason Long opted to hold onto them.

It took a jury of twelve men two and a half hours to deliberate the case. On May 3, 1938, the foreman of the jury, C. J. Chryst, read the verdict. They found Coston guilty of murder in the first degree. This decision came with a mandatory sentence of death. Coston stated, "The only thing I have to say is that I am innocent of the charge, and had nothing to do with it. I was convicted on the perjured testimony of two men and I am innocent."

An appeal was immediately filed with the Florida Supreme Court. They granted him a new trial that resulted in a mistrial being declared on November 18, 1939.

On February 29, 1940, at his third trial, Coston was found guilty of third degree murder and sentenced to twenty years in the state penitentiary at Raiford. In a way, this was a life sentence for Coston because he died there on September 8, 1942, at the age of fifty-three from a lung abscess.

As for Long and Sykes, they were never brought to trial. The cases against both were dropped in March of 1940.

Arrested for Eating Soup Loudly

1923

Thirty-four-year-old Isaac Hirschorn was arraigned on charges of disorderly conduct in Essex Market Court on December 15, 1923. The reason? He was loud and boisterous while eating a bowl of soup at a restaurant located at 25 St. Mark's Place.

Hirschorn claimed that he wasn't being disorderly—that was the way he always ate his soup. Although he did apologize, he felt that he was unable to avoid making noise while eating his soup.

Magistrate McAndrews dismissed the charges, but told Hirschorn, "Eat your soup at home in the future and the other courses of your meal in a restaurant. You are discharged."

Kidnapper Rides on Car Hood in Nightgown

1964

A woman in a nightgown was seen clinging to the front of an automobile as it was being driven down the road. If your first thought was that the woman's life was in great danger and that the car should have been stopped, well, you would be wrong.

Imagine this: A car is driving through Spartanburg, South Carolina, with a young woman clad only in a white nightgown on its hood. An estimated twenty-car caravan is trailing behind, trying to stop the driver. While this may seem like fiction, it really did happen on Monday, August 17, 1964.

It all started around 11:30 p.m. the Sunday night prior in Kannapolis, North Carolina. Twenty-six-year-old Grady Lee Steen was at a drive-in restaurant with his girlfriend, Patsy Queen, when a car drove up beside them. Twenty-three-year-old Joyce Kaye LaFevers exited the car, walked up to Steen, and asked to speak with him alone. When Miss Queen refused to get out of the car, Steen told LaFevers that she should get in, too.

Miss LaFevers got into the back seat, pulled a gun out from under her skirt, and ordered Miss Queen to exit the vehicle. She then ordered Steen to follow the car that LaFevers had arrived in, which was now being driven by twenty-five-year-old Stacey LaVern Bigham. They drove to a nearby service station where Steen was ordered to get into Bigham's car.

The three then drove to Charlotte, North Carolina, where Steen was forced to call Kannapolis police and let them know that he had not been kidnapped and that everything was fine. A stop was then made at a nearby motel where LaFevers and Bigham picked up their clothing. From there, they drove to Douglas Municipal Airport in Charlotte and rented a car, leaving their vehicle behind.

They then started driving toward Atlanta. Upon reaching Spartanburg, they rented a room at the Howard Johnson Motel.

The two robbed Steen of a $130 check, plus $4 that he had in cash. Bigham, who wished to purchase an airplane, threatened to kill Steen if he did not come up with an additional $5,000 ($41,000 today). LaFevers's request was straightforward: either Steen married her or she would kill him. "If I can't have you, then nobody else will," Steen later quoted her as saying.

At 3:00 a.m., Bigham fell sleep. Steen continued to talk to LaFevers until she went to bed at around 5:00 a.m. While the two kidnappers slept, Steen grabbed the car keys and pistol and quietly exited the room around 6:00 a.m.

Steen jumped in the car and quickly locked the doors, but the slamming of the car door awoke LaFevers. Unable to get into the car, she threw her body across its hood. Steen proceeded to slowly drive away, fearing that excessive speed would cause her to fall off the hood.

LaFevers begged to be let into the car. When Steen refused, she ripped off the side view mirror and smashed the windshield with it.

The sight of this scantily clad woman riding on the hood of a car caught motorists by surprise, and many began to follow Steen's vehicle. One motorist pulled up beside Steen and pointed at the young woman on his hood, but Steen kept on going. He traveled slowly as an ever-growing line of cars trailed behind him. This caught the attention of officers and when Steen stopped at another traffic light on Magnolia Street, they jumped out and surrounded the car.

LaFevers slid down off the hood of the car and charged right at Steen. Arresting officer J. G. Tate stated, "She was down and clawing at him in a hurry. We pulled her off and put her in the patrol car but she wouldn't tell us a thing."

The three bewildered policemen were unsure of what had really happened. While Steen claimed that he had been kidnapped, his story seemed unbelievable. As a result, both Steen and LaFevers were arrested. Eventually, Steen was able to convince police that his story was true. Officers then went to the Howard Johnson Motel and arrested Bigham.

Soon after Bigham was taken into custody, other inmates began to request that the jailer allow them to pay off their fines. It was soon determined that Bigham had cashed Steen's $130 check and distributed the money to the inmates.

Bigham and LaFevers were both sentenced to four-year terms in federal prison for the kidnapping.

Woman Bites Dog

1941

Two women stood before Los Angeles Municipal Court Judge Orfa Jean Shontz on November 6, 1941, in what initially seemed to be an ordinary case. Mrs. Sophie Koshelnik had been bitten by a dog owned by Ms. Rose Wolf. Koshelnik was seeking $50 ($860 today) in damages.

As Mrs. Koshelnik explained what had happened, she shocked Judge Shontz when she stated, "Just because I bit the dog, the cur turned around and sunk his teeth in my lip."

"What did you say?" Judge Shontz questioned. "It sounded like you said you bit the dog."

"That's right, your honor," Mrs. Koshelnik replied. "But it was all a mistake." She explained that she had been playing with the dog. When it began to growl, bark, and snap its teeth at her, Mrs. Koshelnik decided to do the same in return. She growled. She barked. She snapped her teeth. "Imagine my surprise when I found I had bit the dog on his nose." The dog was equally surprised and bit her on the lip.

The judge awarded Mrs. Koshelnik $10 ($172 today) and advised that she avoid biting dogs in the future.

The Flying Bandits

1957

The unusual story of two high-flying aviators who attempted to pull off the perfect crime.

On Thursday, October 24, 1957, two drunk men landed a small airplane on a field just outside of Fort Meade, Florida. They proceeded to walk down Broadway before entering the local drug store. After purchasing a couple of pairs of sunglasses, the two then used the payphone located at the front of the store.

The taller of the two men called the local police department, which was located directly across the street. He asked to speak to the police chief but was informed that he had gone home for lunch. When he questioned to whom he was speaking, the person on the other end replied, "This is Constable Harry Godwin."

"Well, Constable Godwin, you better get down here on East Broadway. Couple men acting drunk and mighty disorderly."

The two men, dressed in coveralls, then walked into the street as Godwin drove up alongside them and got out of his patrol car. Observing that the men were clearly intoxicated, Godwin stated, "You're under arrest," to which one of the men replied, "We don't think so—you're the one under arrest."

One of the men shoved the muzzle of a gun into Godwin's left side as the other pressed a gun into his right. They then took Godwin's gun and watch before forcing him to drive a short distance to a wooded area. One of the men stated, "You don't think we mean business, do you?" To emphasize his point, the man brought the gun near Godwin's face, shot a round into the air, and then asked again whether or not Godwin thought they meant business. Godwin replied, "Yes, sir, I do."

Next, they forced the constable to drive back into town. Their destination was the First State Bank of Fort Meade, located on the corner of Broadway and French Avenue. The plan was to enter the bank at 12:58, two minutes prior to the bank's 1:00 p.m. closing.

1910 image of the First State Bank of Fort Meade.

While en route to the bank, Godwin tried his best to attract attention to the potential robbery. Upon spotting a city truck, he swung his police car into its path, but the driver pulled aside and allowed him to pass. Next, he attempted to pull into the path of an approaching car at an intersection, but once again the other driver gave way.

Once they reached the bank, the two men placed stockings over their heads, put on gloves, slipped on their newly purchased sunglasses, and forced Godwin to enter with them. Godwin attempted to draw attention by placing his hands high in the air. In response, one of the bandits blurted out an expletive and said, "You tryin' to give us away? Put your hands down."

Two customers about to enter the bank were herded inside by the bandits as one of them held onto Godwin by his belt and firmly pressed the barrel of the gun against the back of his head.

Twenty-two-year-old assistant cashier Morris R. Lunn was the first to spot the bandits. "I saw them come in the door. They were pushing the constable around some." He continued, "I heard one of them say something. I asked him what he said. I didn't have to ask him what he wanted. I could see that."

Regarding the taller of the two men, Lunn stated, "He threw a sack at me and told me to fill it up." He added, "He was roughing up the constable then. I told all the tellers to get their money out of the drawers and put it into the sack." One of the gunmen then screamed at the female clerks, "You all start shoveling money into the bag or I'll blow his goddamn brains out."

Lunn was then handed a second sack and instructed not to "put [in] anything less than tens." As Lunn turned around, one of the bandits hit him on the back of the head and he fell to the floor. "After I came to, I rolled away from the door as soon as I thought it was safe enough to move. I thought he might come by and see me and think he might as well finish me off."

At around the six-minute mark, the shorter of the bandit pair began to exit from the bank and told his companion, "Come on. What are you trying to do, put on a show for them?" As his partner backed out, he fired a warning shot into a window sash to keep everyone at bay. Leaving Constable Godwin behind inside the bank, the two jumped into his car and sped away.

J. H. White, the bank's vice president and general manager, was returning from an errand when he learned from workmen outside that the bank was being robbed. He shouted the news of the heist down the street to a hardware store employee who, in turn, contacted the police department dispatcher.

By the time Police Chief Glenn Baggett arrived at the bank, the robbery had ended. "I got the call. When I drove up there I didn't know just what to do at first. I didn't see anything going on. Then I heard a car squall down the way. I saw it was Harry's car. I thought 'Harry's on them. There will be one heck of a race now.'"

Baggett continued, "They overshot Bowling Green Road. That's the first indication I had that Harry wasn't in the car. Then I saw two men who had something on their face. They got out of the car and went over the fence. They had a bag." He raced down the road and saw that the two men were attempting to board a small yellow plane.

Fort Meade wholesale fruit dealer Perry Johnson joined in on the chase and arrived on the scene a few seconds later. Baggett stated, "I got out the pump gun, but the shell wouldn't pump into it. I gave it to Perry Johnson and used my pistol." He continued, "I emptied my gun at them. I don't know, but I think Johnson fired three times. They started shooting back."

As one of the bandits climbed aboard the aircraft, the other pulled on the propeller to start the engine. He then climbed aboard as the plane made a quick turn before leaving the ground.

A search both in the air and on the ground commenced within minutes. It was soon learned that a yellow Aeronca airplane had been stolen earlier that morning from the Gilbert Airfield in Winter Haven, some 20 miles (32 km) northeast of Fort Meade. Around 2:00 p.m., a military plane spotted the Aeronca on the ground at the airport in Plant City, about 25 miles (40 km) northwest of the crime scene.

Bullet holes in the Aeronca confirmed to investigators that it was the plane used in the robbery, but they were puzzled as to why the footprints left behind went just a short distance before coming to a sudden stop. After interviewing witnesses, it was established that the two men had abandoned the Aeronca and continued their escape in a smaller, silver Cessna with yellow trim.

A review of aeronautical records indicated that there were only two airplanes registered within the entire state of Florida that matched the description of that silver Cessna. One of them was quickly ruled out. When the owner of the second plane heard that the police were looking for his Cessna, he immediately made contact with authorities. He told them that earlier in the day, he had lent the airplane to an employee named Donald J. Thompson who needed it to attend to some urgent business in Venice, Florida.

Thompson was an immediate suspect, but nothing about him suggested that he would take part in a bank robbery. "Bugs" Thompson was a skilled ex-military pilot who had flown in many Florida airshows. Shortly after World War II he married his wife Barbara, and they were the proud parents of a seven-year-old daughter named Donna.

At 5:06 p.m., Thompson landed the Cessna at Tampa International and was immediately arrested. He admitted that he had been drinking, but emphatically denied any involvement in the Fort Meade robbery.

Coincidentally, a few minutes prior to Thompson's arrest, there was a collision between two automobiles at the corner of Cypress Street and Howard Avenue in Tampa. Police became suspicious of one of the drivers—twenty-six-year-old Irving U. Suits—after learning that he was both an airplane broker and in possession of $305 in cash ($2,750 today). While he was being escorted off to the city jail, a further search of his vehicle uncovered two sets of coveralls similar to those used in the holdup.

Both Suits and Thompson were placed in police lineups. Two employees of the Fort Meade drugstore positively identified both men as the two that had bought sunglasses earlier in the day, establishing that the suspects had been in Fort Meade prior to the robbery. Yet Constable Godwin was only able to pick Suits out of the lineup.

Faced with all of the mounting evidence, Suits admitted to his part in the crime. He named Thompson as his co-conspirator, but Thompson steadfastly denied any involvement. Thompson admitted that he had been drinking and that he had given Suits flying lessons earlier in the day, but said he knew nothing about the bank robbery.

Suits told investigators that the robbery had been planned for several weeks. Fort Meade was chosen because it was a small town with a small police force. After the gun battle in Fort Meade, the two had flown to Plant City to ditch the Aeronca. They then piloted the smaller Cessna to an abandoned airstrip on Boca Grande Island, where they hid the loot. From there, they flew to Peter O. Knight Airport in Tampa, where Suits got out. Thompson refueled and then lifted off for Tampa

International Airport to return his boss's airplane. Suits crashed the car while he was driving to Tampa International to pick up Thompson and complete the final step in their grand escape.

When asked about the location of the loot, Suits stated, "I was so drunk at the time that I really am a little hazy about the entire matter. I don't know whether or not I can take you to where those suitcases are." On Friday, October 25th, two Coast Guard helicopters flew the search party and Suits to Boca Grande, and the hunt began. Twenty-five hours after the robbery had occurred, the two suitcases were located. One contained a pillowcase stuffed with the cash, while the other contained .32-caliber ammunition, a pair of coveralls, and a pair of shoes. All but $69 of the $26,657 stolen (over $240,000 today) had been accounted for.

And yet, Bugs Thompson stood by his story. He insisted that he had nothing to do with the crime. It was only after being confronted with all of the evidence gathered by investigators that he finally admitted to his role in the holdup on Saturday. Now that both men had confessed to the crime, they were asked to escort officers to the location where they had discarded Constable Godwin's gun. As they left the jail, Thompson reportedly snapped at Suits, "Why did you tell them where the money was? You could have told them anything but that. That's what we did it for—the money."

The two were hauled into court on Tuesday, October 29, but declined to enter a plea until they had consulted with a lawyer. Suits told Judge Roy H. Amidon, "If I can ever be given another chance I swear there will never be another drop of alcohol in my house. I vow that before God." He added, "I want to apologize to everyone for the trouble I've caused—the way I let my wife down and to my folks and to everyone concerned."

On November 25, 1957, both pleaded guilty to the charges. Suits' attorney J. H. Willson requested leniency, pointing out that his client had "freely admitted his guilt" and that he had helped investigators recover all of the money. Judge Amidon wasn't buying any of this. "I am really sorry for your situation," he told the defendants. "You have the potentialities of making good citizens, and you have shown a good attitude. We don't need men like you in the penitentiary." However, he added that they "chose a crime which requires a stiff penalty."

He sentenced Suits and Thompson to fifteen years each in state prison for the bank robbery, plus an additional fifteen each for robbing Constable Godwin of his car, gun, and watch. Both sentences were to be served concurrently. Two days later, the two were in federal court where US District Judge Barker added on another fifteen years to each of their sentences, to be served in tandem with their state sentence.

While in prison, Irvin Urton Suits divorced his first wife. Upon his release, he remarried two additional times. He passed away on July 10, 1998, at sixty-seven years of age.

Donald Jerome Thompson would see a more tragic end. He was training Dr. Paul D. Cope to fly the night of October 23, 1971, when Cope's twin-engine Beechcraft Baron crashed while taking off from St. Petersburg-Clearwater International Airport at around 7:30 p.m. Thompson, his wife Barbara, Dr. Cope, and his son Charles, all lost their lives that evening.

PART 2

ENTREPRENEURS
& DARING MINDS

She Dared to Wear Slacks

1938

Today, we take for granted the fact that women can wear slacks any day and everywhere. Helen Hulick was one of those women who fought for their right to do so.

On Wednesday, November 9, 1938, twenty-eight-year-old kindergarten teacher Helen Hulick was in Los Angeles Municipal Court testifying against two men accused of burglarizing her home. As she waited to be called, Judge Arthur S. Guerin summoned Detective Lieutenants William G. Baird and G. W. Sullivan to the bench and told them that Miss Hulick would need to change into clothing more appropriate for a courtroom.

The problem was that Hulick had chosen to wear blue flannel slacks that day. It wasn't the blue color that the judge found offensive. It was the slacks themselves. She dared to wear, as the judge stated, "pants" in his courtroom.

A bail bondswoman generously offered to loan her a skirt, but Hulick refused. She stated, "Certainly not. I'm properly clothed. No judge can tell me to wear a skirt. I like slacks. They're comfortable. It is my constitutional right to wear 'em."

Judge Guerin was visibly annoyed by the young teacher's indignant attitude. "I don't set styles. But costumes acceptable at the beach are not acceptable in formal courtroom procedure. Slacks are not the proper attire in court. It's tough sometimes to be a judge."

It was not in their clients' best interest to have an angry judge and an uncooperative witness, so the defense motioned to postpone the hearing. The judge agreed and rescheduled the hearing for November 14th. He stated, "When the young woman returns, then I'll be prepared to test just how far I can go in maintaining the dignity in my courtroom."

When Monday rolled around, Hulick again refused to obey and strolled into the courtroom donning a pair of orange-and-green slacks. She was accompanied by her attorney, William Katz, who lugged in four thick law books containing citations relevant to his client's right to dress as she pleased.

November 14, 1938, image of Helen Hulick wearing slacks to court.

Judge Guerin was outraged. "The last time you were in this court dressed as you are now and reclining on your neck on the back of your chair, you drew more attention from spectators, prisoners, and court attaches than the legal business at hand. You were requested to return in garb acceptable to courtroom procedure."

"Today you come back dressed in pants and openly defying the court and its duties to conduct judicial proceedings in an orderly manner. It's time a decision was reached on this matter and on the power the court has to maintain what it considers orderly conduct."

"The court hereby orders and directs you to return tomorrow in accepted dress. If you insist on wearing slacks again you will not be prevented from testifying because that would hinder the administration of justice. But be prepared to be punished according to the law for contempt of court."

As Hulick exited the courtroom, she told the press, "Listen. I've worn slacks since I was fifteen. I don't own a dress except a formal. If he wants me to appear in a formal gown that's okay with me." She added, "I'll come back in slacks and if he puts me in jail I hope it will help to free women forever of anti-slackism."

Fast forward twenty-four hours and Hulick was seated directly across from the two men who had robbed her. As she removed her brown-and-gray plaid coat, it was immediately clear that she had once again gone against the judge's request. Underneath, she was wearing a pair of gray-green slacks with a red-and-white blouse.

As the saying goes, three strikes and you're out. This was clearly not going to end well. One could hear a pin drop as those in the courtroom awaited Judge Guerin's entrance. Surprisingly, he said nothing about Hulick's appearance as she gave her testimony, which resulted in the two men being bound for trial.

And then the judge let loose on Helen Hulick. He was fully prepared, with seven typewritten pages outlining her offense against the court. The judge wrote that she had appeared in "a tight-fitting sweater and tight-fitting pants, commonly known as slacks," and that the "effect of this on the orderly procedure of the court was not acceptable." As to Hulick's claim that she could dress as she pleased, he responded, "According to your argument, nudists might enter the court unclothed because they felt more comfortable that way."

"It is the opinion of this court that by disobeying its orders regarding proper attire, your conduct has been contemptuous, tending to bring the court into disrepute." He continued, "Your conduct, in the face of two warnings, has been flagrantly and openly contemptuous. Therefore it is the duty of this court to impose the maximum sentence under the law, which is five days in jail."

Hulick was then taken to the county jail, where she was booked, fingerprinted, and forced to change into a blue denim dress. One hour later, she was released on a writ of habeas corpus. She wasted no time in climbing out of that dress and back into her slacks.

Next stop: the appellate court.

Two days later, on November 17, 1938, two judges listened intently to both sides as they attempted to settle once and for all this argument over women wearing slacks in the courtroom.

Attorney Katz argued at length that Hulick was well within her rights to wear slacks in a courtroom. It was not for the courts to decide which fashions were acceptable, nor should someone be imprisoned simply because a judge does not approve of their style.

The opposition argued that this was not a debate over whether one could wear slacks or not. The real issue was Hulick's attitude. She repeatedly defied the judge's orders and had a "leering and contemptuous expression on her face."

A decision was handed down the next day. The court wrote, "While the court record indicates by way of recital that petitioner in a court room during proceedings indulged in a type of exhibitionism which may have tended to impede orderly procedure, and which she might have been required to discontinue on pain of disciplinary action, the commitment appears to be based solely on petitioner's failure to obey the judge's order to change her attire, which attire, so far as the record before us discloses, did not of itself interfere with orderly court procedure, but involved merely a question of taste, a matter not within the court's control."

Helen Hulick had won. The court ordered that her five-day sentence be absolved and that she be set free.

In response, Judge Guerin seemed quite accepting of the decision. "In meeting the issue, I have considered my duty as a judge in deciding the matter that came before me." He continued, "I accept the decision as final and will be guided by it in the future."

An editorial in the November 21, 1938, publication of the *Los Angeles Times* disagreed. The author wrote, in part, that "the appellate division of the local Superior Court seems rather to have missed the point." They continued, "It was not her attire but her repeated defiance of the court which constituted the contempt."

"Probably most people will consider she had well earned the punishment. She is a schoolteacher and one of her functions is, or should be, to inculcate in her youthful charges a sense of discipline and respect for constituted authority, irrespective of whether or not their juvenile minds may always be in accord with rules so laid down. One wonders to what extent her own attitude and example contribute to her professional qualifications."

On January 17, 1939, Hulick was back in court to testify at the trial of the two accused men. This time she arrived in what was described as "a close-fitting, rust silk dress, sheer hose, high-heeled shoes and a pert up tilting hat with flowing veil."

"Maybe there's something to this dressing-up business after all," Helen told the members of the press. "Because I've been stepping out every night since I decided to dress like the rest of the girls."

January 17, 1939, image of Helen Hulick wearing a dress to court.

The Wheelbarrow Man

1878

In the 1870s, newspapers were the blogs of the day.
Almost daily, they reported on the Wheelbarrow Man as
he made his way along his journey.

When the "Last Spike" of the First Transcontinental Railroad
was driven into the ground at Promontory Point, Utah, on May
10, 1869, travel time across the United States was reduced from
six months to just one week. Yet few could afford the fare—
though a bench seat in third class could be obtained for as little
as $65 ($1,240 today), it was still out of reach for many people.
Travel by wagon was the best alternative, but travel was slow
and road conditions were poor.

One man offered up a more unique way to cross the country.
His name was R. Lyman Potter, and he proposed to do so by
pushing a wheelbarrow from his home in Albany, New York, all
the way to San Francisco, California. A widower and father to
three children, Potter was considered to be a bit of an eccentric.
For example, when Ulysses S. Grant was elected president of
the United States, Potter declared that he would not shave

his face or cut his hair until a Democrat was elected into office. In keeping his word, he allowed his dark brown hair to extend below his shoulders and his beard to grow nearly equal in length.

Potter described how the idea to push a wheelbarrow across the country came about: "Waal, it all came from too damn much talk. We wus talkin' about work and earnin' money, and hard times, etc., and I said I'd wheel a wheelbarrow to San Francisco for a dollar a day rather'n be without work. The Albany fellows took me up and made up $1,000 [$26,300 today], which is now on deposit in Albany. I had nothin' to do and as I wouldn't back down, I started out and here I am."

The rules set down were straightforward: Potter was to trundle his wheelbarrow 4,085 miles (6,574 km) from Albany to San Francisco within 215 working days. They stipulated that he could not travel on Sundays, nor could he take advantage of any other form of transportation to help him along the way.

Potter's wheelbarrow was constructed especially for the trip. It differed little from the typical wheelbarrow of the day—wooden wheel and all—except that his was lighter in design and carried a wooden box atop its frame.

At 3:00 p.m. on April 10, 1878, thirty-seven-year-old Potter began his long trek in the pouring rain. He had just $3.55 ($93.00 today) in his pocket. Potter carried minimal supplies with him: a rubber coat, a change of underwear, camping supplies, and some medications for his feet.

It's about a fifteen-minute drive from my house to downtown Albany, so I went in search of his exact starting point, which at the time was widely reported to have been the corner of Warren and Swan Streets. This proved to be impossible, as those two streets have never intersected. What is also unclear is how he, an upholsterer, was financially able to leave his family behind for the many months that this walk was anticipated to take.

At the end of his first day, Potter had walked 16 miles (26 km) to Schenectady, New York. He was described as being "footsore, wet, and tired, and somewhat dispirited." Yet, despite the rain, he continued on his way. On the morning of April 15, he entered Utica, New York, completing a total distance of 90 miles (145 km).

The press was starting to take notice of his endeavor, but not in a good way. At various times along his journey, newspapers referred to him as a tramp, an idiot, a brainless fool, and as the "wheelbarrow lunatic." This ridicule infuriated Potter and made him even more determined to make it to his final destination.

Lettering on the sides of his wheelbarrow announced his intentions as he entered each town along the way. "From Albany to San Francisco in 250 days! Sundays out—Started April 10, 1878—Time by R. L. Potter, 215!"

By the time he reached Buffalo, New York, on April 26, he had become a bit of a minor celebrity. A small crowd followed him as he traveled through the city. The press reported on where he ate breakfast, and that he'd made a stop at the post office to see if any mail addressed to him had arrived.

Soon, he was on his way again. From Buffalo, he traveled along the southern shore of Lake Erie. His passage through Pennsylvania was brief, with a cursory mention in the press that he had stopped in Erie. He soon crossed into Ohio and headed for Cleveland.

Up until this point, his travel had been along the turnpikes, which hardly resemble the paved roads of today. As he headed farther west and the population dwindled, he would be forced to walk along passageways that barely qualified as roads. When even those passageways were unavailable, Potter traveled along railbeds that greatly hindered his ability to smoothly push his wheelbarrow.

It would have been very easy for Potter to cheat, so he documented his travels by having people write in a book that he carried with him. One entry read, "I saw Mr. R. Lyman Potter at Monroeville, O. I left town about five or eight minutes after Mr. Potter started and trotted one mile and a half before I overtook him. I rode aside him for four and a half miles, and found it quite difficult to keep up with him without trotting. I have a fast walking mare. Mr. Potter is a very sociable man and seems to be a very good man. He stayed at my house the night of the 13th of May. Wm. T Marion, Providence, Lucas County, Ohio."

As he traveled, his story was picked up by newspapers nationwide, and Potter capitalized on his newfound fame. Businesses paid him to advertise on signs affixed to the sides of his wheelbarrow. Others were willing to pay for his food and lodging. He even acted as a mailman, charging for each letter that he delivered. "Every one [*sic*] on the road was very kind to me, and would not, many times, take any money from me. I took letters to deliver on my way at two bits each, and got quite a mail-bag."

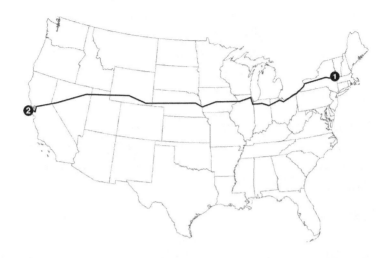

Approximate route that R. Lyman Potter would take from Albany, NY (1) to San Francisco, CA (2).

A man pushing a wheelbarrow would cause little excitement today, but in 1878, Potter's arrival in a town was a major event. For example, when he arrived in Fort Wayne, Indiana, on May 16, a month after his start date, he was greeted at the train depot by a number of dignitaries and tendered freedom of the city.

He penned the following letter on May 19 (his thirty-ninth day of travel): "I arrived at Columbia City at 9.10 this p.m. Am well and in good condition." He concluded, "Please answer at Chicago Ills. Yours &c, R. Lyman Potter."

Potter was nine days ahead of schedule when he entered Chicago on May 23 and remained there for three days. The *Globe-Democrat* reported, "The wheelbarrow idiot, R. Lyman Potter, arrived in this city this morning. He is represented as being the most dilapidated looking biped that has worn shoe leather in these parts for a considerable period."

Next up was the state of Iowa. "He may be expected to pass through Council Bluffs and Omaha in due course of time, unless some friend of humanity kills him before he gets there." Potter safely reached Council Bluffs on June 21, and was then approximately 1,200 miles (1,931 km) from home.

Nebraska offered Potter his first real setback. "After I left Chicago, I did not stop more than a day or two anywhere on the route, except at Plum Creek, Nebraska, where I had sunstroke, which laid me out for fifteen days."

While in North Platte, Nebraska, on July 14 (day ninety-five), he penned the following letter to the editor of the *Fort Wayne Sentinel*: "Good health. Feel happy. Hoping this will find you same. Going every day and confident I'll make it. Very hot weather, which don't agree for a long journey. Write, Ogden, San Francisco and Sacramento. R. L. Potter."

Upon reaching Cheyenne, Wyoming, on July 26, it was reported that Potter was "met in the outskirts of the town by a delegation of citizens who extended to him the freedom of the city, which he accepted. When the officials and dignitaries of the camp got through with him, the hoodlums, who were abound there, got hold of him and filled him up with budge, and before he was in the Magic City an hour he was as incoherent as the pages of the *Pioneer*."

In another letter penned to the *Sentinel*, Potter wrote: "Laramie City, W. T. [Wyoming Territory], July 31, 1878.—I feel as good and as healthy as I ever did. Hope this will find you the same. Had a breakdown twice on the road, plenty of snow in part of the country. I remain yours respectfully, R. L. Potter."

Potter passed through Utah in late August and spent most of September in Nevada. Upon entering California, passage over the Sierra Nevada range proved difficult, as he was forced to travel over a seemingly endless succession of railroad ties. His wheelbarrow bounced up and down in a rhythmic pattern as he moved closer to San Francisco.

He rolled his wheelbarrow down K Street in Sacramento on October 7, as a crowd of hundreds looked on. As he approached his final destination, the *San Francisco Examiner* published the following critique:

> A few days ago there passed through a town in Oregon an old negro, 70 years of age, and of 300 pounds weight, on his way to Puget Sound. He had walked all the way from Louisiana; but he pushed no wheelbarrow, had no money staked on his performance, nor did he make any pretentious display of himself because of his really extraordinary feat in pedestrianism. He started on the long journey for the purposes of getting employment, and he certainly deserves it at good wages for the remainder of his days. If there is any celebrity or reward due to either of the two, to the tough and resolute old negro ought it to be given.

The following announcement appeared in newspapers across the country: "San Francisco, October 15.—R. Lyman Potter, the wheelbarrow man, arrived about noon to-day [*sic*]. The crowd followed him through the streets." The next day's papers wrote, "The arrival of the wheelbarrow man was an advertising hoax. Potter will not be here for a day or two."

He pushed on to Oakland, but the rules established back in Albany prohibited him from directly crossing the bay into San Francisco. He had no choice but to walk along the waterway's perimeter. He headed southward toward San Jose before turning northward toward San Francisco.

Finally, on October 27, 1878, Potter and his wheelbarrow entered San Francisco as police and a brass band escorted him down Mission Street. Upon arriving at Woodward's Gardens, a popular amusement venue where he had been hired to appear, he was greeted by a crowd estimated to be between 12,000 and 15,000 people.

It had been 201 days since Potter left Albany. While in Sacramento, he was asked the total cost of the trip. He commented, "About $300 [$7,900 today]. Meals were very expensive, four bits [fifty cents] and $1."

Surprisingly, Potter had still not met all of the conditions laid out in that original $1,000 bet. He was required to walk 4,085 miles, yet he had only covered 3,995 miles upon his arrival in San Francisco. He would accrue the additional 90 miles during his daily performances at Woodward's Gardens.

Potter's final day at Woodward's Gardens was on November 11. On the 20th, it was announced in the newspapers that forty-one-year-old Leon Pierre Federmeyer had challenged Potter to a transcontinental wheelbarrow race. On December 8, 1878, at 3:45 p.m., the two set out for New York on a $1,500 wager ($39,450 today).

Passage through the mountains was made treacherous by sub-zero temperatures and incredible depths of snow. Potter and Federmeyer remained neck-and-neck until they reached Battle Mountain, Nevada, on January 12, 1879, where Potter became ill and began to fall behind. From that point on, Potter seemed more focused on cashing in on his fame than winning the race. He spent two months in Leadville, Colorado, and argued that Federmeyer had forfeited the race by riding in a wagon for 23 miles (37 km) and skipping Salt Lake City, which cut 80 miles (129 km) off his trip.

With each passing day, Federmeyer pulled farther ahead, though it wasn't all smooth sailing. While passing over the Sierra, his left foot froze in the extreme cold. In Sheridan, Kansas, he fell 15 feet (4.6 m) and struck the rocks below. Federmeyer arrived in New York on July 24, 1879—229 days after departing from San Francisco.

At the time of Federmeyer's arrival, Potter was still somewhere back in Illinois. By this point, he had started making money displaying the large number of curiosities he had collected over the course of his travels. Those willing to pay would see a variety of dried snakes and other specimens, and could peruse through his books filled with postal marks and other evidence of the places he'd visited. Most interestingly, he tamed a live wolf cub that then rode atop the box of his wheelbarrow.

He spent the winter of 1881 in Baltimore, Maryland, and may have returned to Albany after that to see his family, but exact details are unclear.

In late 1882, Potter set out from New York on a wager that he could get to New Orleans within a given amount of time. When it became clear that he wouldn't make it, his backers pulled their funding and left Potter nearly penniless. Having just reached Tennessee, he turned back toward home.

Potter arrived in Salisbury, North Carolina, on Friday, March 30, 1883. He left around noon and followed the Richmond and Danville railroad track northward. Upon reaching the bridge over the Yadkin River, the watchman refused his passage. Potter was told that he needed to take the ferryboat at a cost of 25 cents ($6.80 today), which he refused to do. Potter returned to Salisbury to request crossing permission from railroad officials but was denied. He spent the next hour drinking whisky and was drunk by the time he left town.

The lifeless body of R. Lyman Potter was found near the track the next morning, about 1.5 miles (2.4 km) east of town. A coroner's jury concluded that he was standing too close to the track when a train passed. As the train brushed past him, Potter was knocked to the ground and killed.

Potter was buried in Salisbury, and all of his personal effects were sent back to his wife in Albany. His wheelbarrow was described as being in the most dilapidated state, with its wheel bound together by endless windings of knotted rope. His wheelbarrow, with its "one thousand curiosities," was estimated to weigh 240 pounds (109 kg). Found among his possessions were letters from his family begging him to come home.

At the time of his death, the United States still had a Republican president and Potter's hair remained uncut. A Democrat would not occupy the White House until Grover Cleveland assumed the office in 1885.

A King Without a Country

1893

Just what would you do if you found a remote island that belonged to no country and that no person lived on? When James Harden-Hickey stumbled across the uninhabited Atlantic island of Trinidad, he claimed it as his own.

Located on the border between Egypt and its southern neighbor, Sudan, lies a small sliver of the African continent to which neither country lays claim. Known as Bir Tawil, this isolated, land-locked, 795-square-mile (2,059-square-kilometer) trapezoidal strip of desert is home to no one and of little value to either country.

To understand why Bir Tawil remains unclaimed, it is important to mention another piece of land known as the Hala'ib Triangle. Located to the northeast of Bir Tawil, the Hala'ib Triangle is a fertile region that borders the Red Sea and is thought to have valuable oil and mineral resources. As a result, both countries have laid claim to the Hala'ib Triangle, though it is currently under Egyptian control.

On January 19, 1899, an agreement between Egypt and the United Kingdom established the border between Egypt and Sudan as being along the 22nd north line of latitude. Since the Hala'ib Triangle was located above this line of latitude, the valuable piece of land clearly belonged to Egypt. And, since Bir Tawil was below it, the worthless piece of desert was thus in Sudan's hands.

Then, on November 4, 1902, the British drew up a new document that adjusted the boundary based on the actual use of the land by tribes in the area. The new line placed the Hala'ib Triangle under Sudanese control, and Bir Tawil under Egyptian.

And there lies the rub: each country lays claim to the Hala'ib Triangle by citing the respective document that favors it over the other. Should either country claim ownership of Bir Tawil, they would be accepting the agreement that assigned the more valuable Hala'ib Triangle to the other party. Neither wants to do this, so at least for now, Bir Tawil remains a no-man's land.

If you are thinking of heading to Bir Tawil and staking it as your own (I certainly did for a brief moment), you'd better think twice about doing so. In addition to being nearly inhospitable and inaccessible, the few individuals that have laid claim to it have never been taken seriously by the international community.

But what if you came across another piece of land that no country had claimed? What would you do? Well, before you do anything, you may want to pay careful attention to the story of Baron James Harden-Hickey, who one day happened to stumble across an uninhabited, unclaimed island in the Atlantic Ocean.

To fully understand this little kingdom of Harden-Hickey, you must first know a bit about the man himself: James Aloysius Harden-Hickey was born on December 8, 1854 in San Francisco. His parents were among San Francisco's earliest settlers, his father was of Irish descent and his mother French. The year 1854 was the tail end of the California Gold Rush, and the Wild West was not the best of places to raise a child. When he was eight years old, the decision was made to take James to

France and enroll him in the finest of schools. He would not return to California for another fourteen years.

After completing his basic education, Harden-Hickey enrolled in the University of Namur in Belgium, and after that spent two years studying law at Leipzig University in Germany. Harden-Hickey then enrolled in the military academy at Saint Cyr, graduated with honors, and pursued a career in the French Army.

In 1883, his father passed away and left him with a small inheritance. At this point, he decided to abandon his military career and redirect his attention to sculpting and writing under the pseudonym of Saint Patrice. Angered by Parisian attacks on the Catholic Church, he authored a number of essays and pamphlets seriously defending the faith and, in return for his efforts, was awarded the title of Baron. Between 1876 and 1880, he penned eleven full-length novels.

Baron Harden-Hickey was an ardent Royalist who believed that France would be far better off as a monarchy, a common theme throughout his published works. His writings caught the attention of a small group of Royalists who were planning to publish an illustrated weekly titled *Le Triboulet*. Harden-Hickey was appointed editor, and the first issue was published on November 10, 1878. Attacking the Republic did not go over well with those in power, and the paper faced numerous lawsuits, arrests, and fines.

In an interview with the *San Francisco Chronicle* on April 28, 1887, Harden-Hickey stated, "I have the honor to say we have had over forty actions at law and libel suits during our existence. At first the old French press law was in effect, requiring the cartoons to be submitted to government censors before publication. The censors objected to our cartoons. We published them, nevertheless."

While few would choose it as an option today, dueling was Harden-Hickey's preferred method of settling a debate. When questioned about this in the same interview, he responded, "Yes, I have [had] about a dozen: I think it is ten." He continued, "But really I think it is the better way. Newspapers are then not so ready to attack a man without good cause and public men are more respectful to journalists. Yes, it is better all around."

Because he was not a French citizen, Harden-Hickey was ultimately expelled from the country for his political offenses. His time in exile was spent in Belgium and England, but he eventually snuck back into France and resumed his work at *Le Triboulet*, where he remained until 1888.

It was then that Harden-Hickey decided to make some big changes in his life. He divorced his wife, Countess de Saint-Péry, and hopped aboard the British merchant ship *Astoria* for a two-year journey around the world.

One year of this time was spent in India, where he studied the principles and history of Buddhism. Upon his return to Paris, he took to trashing the Catholic Church and espousing Buddhism in his writings.

In 1890, he met Annie Harper Flagler, who was thirteen years younger than him. The couple married on Saint Patrick's Day of the following year in New York City. Her father, multimillionaire John Haldane Flagler, strongly opposed the marriage. While Annie had inherited a fortune from her late mother, it was her dad who controlled the purse strings. Flagler refused to entrust Harden-Hickey with the care of his wife's money, casting a dark cloud over their marriage for the remainder of the Baron's life.

In 1894, he penned a bizarre 167-page volume titled *Euthanasia: The Aesthetics of Suicide*, in which he discusses and offers up justification for suicide, while describing the best means of doing so—not exactly the most uplifting of reads. At some point he began to reflect upon the meaning of his trip around the world and on November 5, 1893, on the front page of the *New-York Tribune*, Harden-Hickey announced that from that point forward, he was to be referred to as James I, Prince of Trinidad. You may be thinking that he had taken leave of his senses, and maybe he had, but his claim wasn't as absurd as one would initially believe.

James Harden-Hickey, a.k.a. James I, Prince of Trinidad.

It should be pointed out that when he declared himself to be the monarch of Trinidad, he was not referring to the Trinidad in the Caribbean with which you are likely familiar. Instead, the lesser-known Trinidad in question is a volcanic island that lies approximately 680 miles (1,094 km) east of Brazil, and was completely uninhabited at the time of his proclamation. He had stumbled across it while traveling to India aboard the *Astoria*. Why the ship made the unplanned stop there is not recorded. Some say that the layover was made to seek shelter from a storm, while others report that it was to replenish water and stock up on turtle meat. Either way, Harden-Hickey asked to go ashore and, upon hearing that the island was unclaimed by any country, thus claimed it as his own.

It's not that Trinidad was undiscovered—it was first visited in 1502 by Portuguese explorers and subsequently made part of the Portuguese empire, but remained unoccupied. When fifty-two people aboard the *HMS Rattlesnake* became shipwrecked on the island on October 21, 1781, Commander Philippe d'Auvergne claimed the island for Great Britain. After they were rescued in December 1782, there were no additional long-term residents on the island prior to Baron Harden-Hickey's arrival.

Harden-Hickey told the *Tribune* reporter, "I propose to take possession of the Island of Trinidad under a maxim of international law which declares that anybody may seize and hold waste land that is not claimed by anybody else. The island is uninhabited, and has been so for more than a hundred years. Two or three centuries ago the Portuguese attempted to colonize it, probably by a penal colony. They soon gave up the attempt, however. The English also once made a feeble effort to plant a colony upon it, but the project was abandoned after a short settlement. The remains of these early settlements may still be seen upon the island. No one, however, has lived on it for more than a century."

One of the Baron's first steps was to set up a chancellery for his new nation, initially located at his Manhattan residence on 18 West 52nd Street. He called upon an old friend, Count de la Boissière, to be his minister of foreign affairs. The chancellery was soon moved to a more formal location at 217 West 36th Street, but "formal" may be a bit of an exaggeration. Affixed to the front door was a piece of paper upon which de la Boissière had handwritten: Chancellerié de la Principaute de Trinidad. Inside was a bare, stark interior that consisted of an old desk covered in wrapping paper, a few beat-up chairs, a second-hand bookcase, and an oilcloth that covered the floor—definitely not what one imagines as an office for nobility.

Harden-Hickey penned a four-page prospectus to convince others to invest in his island venture. Still clinging to his Royalist beliefs, he decided that the new nation of Trinidad would be a military dictatorship, with himself as its head honcho. For one to become a colonist of the island, there were two main requirements: first, one had to be white; and second, one had to have high social standing and be able to purchase twenty 1,000 franc bonds. This fee would cover the cost of passage from San Francisco to Trinidad and include the return passage as well, should one wish to go back to the States after one year. The earliest colonists formed an aristocracy, and those appointed as officers were required to wear a mustache.

Harden-Hickey wrote, "I look to the seabirds and the turtles to afford our principal source of revenue. Trinidad is the breeding place of almost the entire feathery population of the South Atlantic Ocean. The exportation of guano alone should make my little country prosperous. Turtles visit the island to deposit eggs and at certain seasons the beach is literally alive with them. The only drawback to my projected kingdom is the fact that it has no good harbor and can be approached only when the sea is calm."

To further entice prospective investors, Harden-Hickey dangled a legend of supposed pirate treasure over their heads. He purported that in 1821, pirates had buried a great quantity of gold and silver on the island that had been plundered from Peruvian churches. Harden-Hickey stated that his newly established government would be willing to split the profits of any buried treasure found with those who discovered it. The government would still, however, retain total control of the island, and all profits made from the sale of guano, and turtle meat and eggs.

To build the necessary docks, buildings, and infrastructure for this budding nation, Harden-Hickey planned to hire five hundred Chinese laborers.

All throughout 1894, Harden-Hickey traveled around the country, attempting to pull this colonization scheme together. He had a jeweler design a royal crown for him to wear. Gold-and-red enamel Crosses of the Order of Trinidad were either awarded or sold. The main source of revenue for this existing-only-on-paper government was raised through the sale of postage stamps, the majority of which were sold to philatelists around the world.

Then, on January 3, 1895, the island of Trinidad was invaded by troops aboard the British warship *Barracouta*. Their intention was to turn this tiny island into a cable station for transatlantic telegraph lines. Of course, to call this an invasion would be a great exaggeration, since the island was guarded by no one. As a result, Harden-Hickey suddenly became a king without a country.

It would be many months before Harden-Hickey became aware that his island had been seized by the British. He dictated a letter of protest, which was written and signed by Count de la Boissière and sent on July 30, 1895, to the United States Department of State. When Secretary of State Richard Olney received the letter, he claimed that he was unable to decipher its messy handwriting. He handed it off to the press, and since they had no problem deciphering de la Boissière's supposed scribble, they published the letter's contents.

Brazil was strongly opposed to the sudden taking of Trinidad and demanded that the British remove their troops from the island. England argued that the island had long been abandoned, so Brazil could no longer lay claim to it.

In an August 2, 1895, interview with the *Los Angeles Times*, Harden-Hickey stated, "Brazil has no claim to the island at all. How can any nation lay claim to an island seven hundred miles from its shores without occupying it? Possession is nine points in international as well as civil law, and as I took possession of the island and occupied it before Brazil or England thought of doing so, I think I have the sole title to it. Brazil, of course, became unduly excited over England's attempted occupation of the island, and it's protest against England's action has helped my cause."

The tug-of-war over Trinidad would continue until January of 1896, when England finally removed their troops. It's not that Brazil had any use for the island—they simply didn't want the British troops so close to their shoreline. It remains under Brazilian control to this day, and they currently have thirty-two navy personnel members stationed there.

On February 9, 1898, after a failed attempt to sell a ranch in Mexico, Harden-Hickey crossed the border and disembarked from his train in El Paso, Texas. He checked in at the Pierson Hotel and retired to his room at around 7:30 that evening. The following morning, 43-year-old Harden-Hickey was found lying upon his bed, stiff as a board. He had committed suicide by consuming an overdose of morphine.

A note to his wife was found pinned to the chair. It read, "My Dearest—No news from you, although you have had plenty of time to write to answer my last. I expect to leave this hotel tomorrow, or the day after. Harvey has written me that he has no one in view for buying my land at present. Well, I shall have drained the cup of bitterness to the very dregs, but I do not complain. I prefer to be a dead gentleman to a living blackguard like your father. Good-by. I forgive your conduct toward me and trust you will be able to forgive yourself. Ever affectionately." It was signed with a name, thought to be a pet name, that no one was able to decipher. Found among his possessions was a copy of his book, *Euthanasia: The Aesthetics of Suicide.*

The Los Angeles Perfume Bombing

1948

Some people will do anything to promote their product, even if that means bombing the city of Los Angeles with perfume.

Supposedly, the cost of the ingredients contained in a bottle of perfume is low when compared to its overall selling price. The packaging, marketing, sales commissions, and profit all combine to drive the cost up. Today, it's estimated that a typical $100 bottle of perfume contains less than $5 worth of ingredients.

It was this high profit margin that attracted two men from Wilton, Connecticut, to the perfume business. The first was N. Lee Swartout, a manager for Swindell Brothers, a manufacturer of glass perfume and prescription bottles. The other was Charles N. Granville, an efficiency engineer. Swartout would later recall, "Charlie had made a survey of a perfume business.

He noticed that it made a high rate of profit. Also, the work didn't seem too hard—mostly a matter of selling the stuff. That combination interested me."

Both men had grown tired of wasting three hours each day aboard a train commuting to their jobs in New York City. It was during one of those evening trips back home that the two hatched a plan to enter the perfume business. By the flip of a coin, Swartout became president of their new endeavor. His first official act was to appoint Granville as treasurer. Each agreed to invest $4,000 ($52,000 today) in starting capital.

Their first order of business was to think of a good name for the company. Since they were living on Skunk Lane at the time, they came up with "The Skunk Works." They used that name informally, and even went as far as donning skunk hats during promotional events, but the name was clearly not ideal for a perfume company. No one wanted to smell like Pepé Le Pew. It was Granville's wife Mary who finally came up with the perfect name. It belonged to a friend of hers who lived in Hammond, Indiana: Angelique Murphy. And so, Angelique and Co. was born.

They came up with what they thought was an ingenious approach to marketing perfume. First, they chose six different product names: Black Satin, Distraction, Est-Est-Est (a wine region in Italy), Folly, Murmur, and Wanderlust. Next, since they had no perfume formulations of their own, they asked the Van Ameringen-Haebler firm—experts in the fragrance field— to develop six for them. Finally, they designed six different styles of packaging. By mixing and matching all of these components, they were able to create an endless set of product combinations that could be personalized for each customer.

Not only did such a variable product line prove to be a logistical nightmare, it was also a marketing failure.

As a result, they decided to simplify. Only one name and one scent would be chosen. Choosing the name was the easiest part—they liked Black Satin best. As for the scent, they asked the people of Wilton to decide for them. They asked the opinion of anyone who was willing to give their perfumes a sniff, and the majority chose one that was "a sultry Oriental blend with overtones of luxury." It also happened to be the costliest of the six formulations to manufacture.

Vintage bottle of Black Satin perfume.

The marketing for Black Satin began in January of 1946. Initially they sold to local stores, but before the year was out, they scored an order with Saks Fifth Avenue in New York City. From that point on, Angelique and Co. grew and grew.

It wasn't that they had an exceptional product—similar perfumes were certainly on the market at the time. What the guys at Angelique excelled at was promotion. Whereas the perfume industry prided itself on exclusivity and sophistication, Angelique focused on the outrageous.

They started off simple. While most perfumes were sampled from testers sitting on countertops in department stores, Angelique developed squirt boxes that could be placed outside of the stores that sold Black Satin. The idea was that potential customers would see the box on the street, press a button to get a little squirt of the perfume, and then enter the store to make a purchase.

Their first big publicity stunt occurred in the winter of 1948. After reading articles in the news about scientists seeding clouds with dry ice to make rain, Granville came up with what was known as "Operation Sweet Snowflake." The plan was simple: have a helicopter fly over Bridgeport, Connecticut, and drop dry ice crystals saturated with Black Satin perfume into the clouds. If all went as planned, scented snow would fall all over the city.

At 11:00 a.m. on February 10, the helicopter lifted off from Bridgeport Municipal Airport. There was barely a cloud in the sky. Fifty pounds (22.7 kg) of the tainted dry ice was dumped into the few clouds that they could find, but not a single snowflake was observed down on the ground. The only thing that fell from the sky that day was Granville's expensive wristwatch—it had accidentally dropped off as he reached his arm out the window of the airplane to seed the cloud. Undaunted, they promised additional attempts in Chicago and Washington, DC, but neither materialized.

Their efforts at making snow may have failed, but they did garner Angelique quite a bit of free nationwide publicity. The press talked about it for days. "Next thing you know," said one weatherman, "someone will be trying to make it snow in colors red, white, and blue, for example, on holidays." A syndicated article joked, "All right, so a Bridgeport citizen comes home reeking of Shocking or Tabu or Chanel No. 5. He tells the little woman he fell in a snowdrift. Does the little woman believe him? Huh!"

The men of Angelique organized their next big promotion in Syracuse, New York. An advertisement in the *Post-Standard* read, "Remember this!...tomorrow, Saturday, March 20, is the date...11 a.m. is the time...in front of The Addis Co. is the place! What's happening...just the most astounding event of the season!...The Easter Bunny arrives by helicopter to deliver a huge Easter egg filled with precious Black Satin to our roof. You won't want to miss seeing him!...you'll certainly want to be present when the delightful scent of Black Satin wafts to the street!"

While having the Easter Bunny come by helicopter was not their most original idea, their next promotional endeavor was the one they'd be best remembered for.

On September 13, 1948, ten Beechcraft Bonanza aircrafts swooped in over Los Angeles and perfume bombed the city. Rest assured that this was no invasion from a foreign country. It was, instead, an invasion led by Angelique's Charlie Granville. He had read up on how officials had tried everything reasonably possible to reduce the city's tear-inducing haze. They fined factories for excessive emissions, cited automobiles that spit out clouds of black soot, and even limited trash burning to specific times of the day, but nothing seemed to help. So Granville offered an alternative solution: he figured that if smog could not be eliminated, it should, at least, be made to smell better.

Granville's plan was simple: a fleet of airplanes would fly over Los Angeles and dispense 75 gallons (284 liters) of Black Satin perfume into the clouds below. Some expressed concern that the scent would never make it through the dense smog and to the ground. "We've asked weather experts about spraying it," Granville responded. "They say that the smell positively will get down."

As an added attraction, Granville hired nine "bombardierettes"—models dressed in full-length pajamas made of, naturally, black satin.

The *Los Angeles Times* reported, "The planes took off from Lockheed Air Terminal, a model in each plane except one. That one carried Charles Granville of Wilton, Ct., one of the perfume company owners. He led the attack to strike the olfactory organs and other strategic targets."

It was claimed that $20,000 ($210,000 today) worth of perfume had been dispensed that day, though that figure has never been officially confirmed. In one sense, this stunt could be considered a total failure. The prevailing winds carried the scented air out to sea, and not a single person reported smelling the perfume down on the ground. Yet, from the Angelique executives' point of view, it was a smashing success. By having the first mass perfume bombing, they received international coverage and their sales increased.

Angelique's next truly big stunt happened in June of 1953. This time they went overseas to Paris, France. Granville's latest plan was to hire an airplane to seed the clouds with a mixture of Black Satin perfume and carbon dioxide. He explained his reasoning, stating, "We're getting tired of American women smelling of French perfume, and so we decided we're going to have French women smell of American perfume whether they like it or not."

Two planes were required. The first carried Granville and his magical rainmaking formula. The second was filled with members of the press, which included famed *Washington Post* humorist Art Buchwald. Did it work? Definitely not, but Black Satin was back in the news.

In 1954, Swartout bowed out of the company and took an early retirement at the age of forty-one. Granville then ran Angelique on his own. Over the years, other formulations such as Pink Satin and Gold Satin were marketed. At one point, the company even attempted to market sachets of wedding rice scented with their floral White Satin perfume. But none proved to be as popular as the original Black Satin.

When Red Satin was introduced, Granville came up with the ultimate promotion. He purchased 300 pounds (136 kg) of red marking dye. His plan was to mix it with their new perfume and have it flow over Niagara Falls. The police caught wind of his plan, however, and prevented him from going through with it.

Now stuck with all that red dye, Granville was unsure of what to do with it. One day, while out on his yacht, he came up with a solution. On July 15, 1959, he launched "Operation Merry Christmas England." A number of boats gathered to spread ten gallons of the perfume mixed with red dye into the water near Miami Beach, Florida. Granville determined that the Gulfstream would carry the scented dye to Great Britain just in time for Christmas. Granville stated, "We expect, among other things, to catch one particular offshoot of the current and perfume Liverpool harbor. Liverpool badly needs something like that." Like all of his other unusual stunts, this one also failed. He later said, "Looks as if it's going to hit New York instead."

Granville seemed to expand his reach with each successive stunt. First he attempted to make scented snow in Connecticut, then he tried to scent the Los Angeles smog, and finally, he attempted to have scented dye travel across the Atlantic Ocean to England. How much bigger could he go?

He had an answer for that: Mars. He wanted to send perfume on the first spaceship sent to the red planet. "There are people on Mars. Some farmer out in Kansas is always reporting that some little green men landed in his wheat field and there's a place down in the Ozarks where people who have seen the little green men hold a convention and tell about seeing them. But what about the little green girls on Mars? Let shoot some perfume their way and maybe we can coax them down for a look."

As crazy as all of Granville's ideas may have been, they achieved the desired goal of free publicity for his company. The first full year that Angelique and Co. was in business, they cleared $169,000 in sales. The following year, they jumped to $320,000. Within six years, they were selling over $1,000,000 of perfume and related products annually.

Sometimes you just need to dream big.

At its peak, Angelique and Co. employed seventy-five people in its Wilton facility. After it was sold to Hazel Bishop-Lanolin Plus, Inc., in October of 1962, the plant was shut down less than four months later. Production was moved to Union, New Jersey, but none of its employees were asked to follow.

PART 3

INEXPLICABLE ODDNESS

Smokin' Bananas

1967

There are some stories that simply make me smile whenever I think about them. This story about people who were smoking banana peels in the 1960s is one of them. It simply borders on the ridiculous.

Years ago my wife was diagnosed with celiac disease, and for one full year, wheat-based products were virtually nonexistent in our home. I was able to live mostly gluten-free myself, but the one food that I truly craved was pizza. Every time my wife was away and I had to dine by myself, I would grab a slice somewhere. In the end, going gluten-free made no difference to my wife's health and I was incredibly happy when further tests confirmed that she did not in fact have celiac disease.

You may be surprised to know that avoiding gluten was originally not the obvious answer when it came to battling celiac disease. Strange as it may seem, the preferred treatment was once to eat lots and lots of bananas. This was based on the research of Dr. Sidney Haas, who published his findings in a 1924 paper titled "The Value of the Banana in the Treatment of Celiac Disease." His "banana and skim milk" diet was to be supplemented with broth, gelatin, oranges, vegetables, and a little meat.

Oddly, the real culprit of celiac disease was staring Dr. Haas right in the face, but he didn't see it. While studying a town in Puerto Rico, he observed that those who ate a large amount of bread suffered from celiac disease, while farmers who lived on a banana-rich diet lacked the symptoms. He concluded that the bananas had some sort of curative power. Not only did his banana diet really save countless lives—mainly because it unintentionally eliminated gluten from the diets of children suffering from celiac disease—but it soon caught on with the general public and became an incredibly popular weight-loss fad.

What's most interesting about this story is that, on the opposite side of the Atlantic, there was another doctor who had also been researching celiac disease as early as 1936. One day, a young mother brought her daughter in for treatment with said doctor and commented that her rash seemed to improve quickly if bread was eliminated from her diet. That doctor was Dr. Willem-Karel Dicke, medical director at the Juliana Children's Hospital in the Hague, and it was then that he realized a wheat-based diet was the cause.

Dr. Dicke published his first paper on wheat-free dieting in 1941. During the Dutch famine of 1944–45, which began when the Germans placed an embargo on all food shipments to the western Netherlands, bread was nearly non-existent. Dicke observed that during that time, many celiac disease symptoms disappeared, providing evidence that grains were somehow the cause of the disease. When the Netherlands was liberated by Allied forces in May of 1945, one of the first foods supplied through a coordinated airdrop was bread, and those suffering from celiac disease saw their symptoms suddenly return.

Dr. Dicke's theory was confirmed through further experiments and soon, doctors all across Europe were recommending the removal of gluten from the diets of those with celiac disease. Yet doctors in the United States were slow to give up the banana diet because it seemed to work, and they continued to recommend it well into the 1960s.

Which leads me to my favorite banana story: the time that smoking banana peels became a national fad.

It remains unclear where the crazy idea to smoke bananas began. Maybe it started on the East Coast, or possibly on the West. Some have argued that the 1967 hit song "Mellow Yellow" by Donovan was about smoking bananas, but that theory has long been debunked. Others say the fad started with Country Joe McDonald, who was supposedly introduced to smoking bananas in mid-February of 1967.

The first known print mention of smoking bananas was an article published in the weekly alternative *Berkeley Barb* on March 3, 1967. "Recipe of the week: Take a banana and eat it, now take the peel and scrape the inside of it until you have a pile of banana pith. Cure the pith in the oven, like grass (i.e. heat it until it crumbles easily) roll it into joints and smoke." Two days later the story was picked up by United Press International (UPI) and within weeks, stoners across the country were giving it a try.

The *Barb's* March 17 issue featured a letter from "Gene Grimm," who wrote that the banana peel contained arterenol, a synthetically-produced chemical used to treat hypertension that can cause hypersensitivity. He served up a warning that it could be harmful "to people under treatment for low blood pressure and low pulse rate." Grimm added, "There is no, or very little, danger that an appreciable amount of the insecticide (2 percent DDT) sprayed on during preharvesting will remain and cause toxic effects. However, if you plan to use the whole peel, wash the outside surface."

In that same issue, a local doctor, who wished to remain anonymous, noted that bananas also contained the neurotransmitter serotonin. "The doctor says if you add a dimethyl ring to serotonin (which may happen when banana skins are baked) a new chemical compound, bufotenine, is created. Bufotenine is a well-known hallucinogen, found in toadstools and toad skins and used by South American Indians."

Trip on a Banana Peel.

Send $5 for your psychedelic turn-on bag to:

Mellow Yellow

2077 Hayes St.,
San Francisco,
Calif. 94117

Mellow Yellow Is Here

April 7, 1967, advertisement for Mellow Yellow banana peel.

In what would be a constant back-and-forth between the believers and the doubters, those of the establishment offered up the following:

Cecil Hider, a chemist at California's Narcotics Bureau, stated, "You can probably take anything and get high if you want to." He added, "But you'll usually get sicker than you will high."

A spokesperson for the Berkeley Police Department denied that their officers were keeping an eye on local fruit markets for large purchases of bananas and added, "We've heard about the banana effect but don't believe it." A San Francisco vice squad inspector commented, "The next thing you know they'll be shooting avocado juice."

A story in the March 24, 1967, *Berkeley Barb* offered up this response to all of the naysayers: "Ha, Ha, Ha, the S. F. Establishment said Mellow Yellow doesn't get you high. About five hundred people got stoned out of their skulls in front of their establishment cameras and no cops (except undercover Narks) in Panhandle Park." The article continued, "The Diggers had about a pound and a half [680 grams] of mellow yellow which was the final result of the 100 pounds [45 kg] of bananas which they processed over the weekend. The bananas cost $20." It concludes, "Yes, we all know the whole thing is totally ridiculous! Except it works!"

***

When the banana peel fad hit the University of Michigan, a junior at the school told the *Detroit Free Press*, "It's the latest thing in this whole business of college students looking for weird drugs." He added that stories of students smoking bananas had spread across campus for a few days, which, in turn, resulted in an increase of banana sales at local groceries.

Another student commented, "Actually, I don't think there's anything special about banana peels. I tried it. I don't think I'd do it again." The student continued, "Most of the kids who try it think it's a joke, but they still go through the motions of preparing it and smoking it as if it were serious business."

In the same article, an unnamed pharmacist that specialized in medicinal plants stated, "If the students really are getting effects like those of LSD, they've discovered something that's not known to scientists." He added, "You could get a funny feeling by smoking anything, including dried lawn grass."

The scariest part of this potential hallucinogen was that it was totally legal. Controlling the supply of bananas would be incredibly difficult. Were police really going to arrest Chiquita Banana and charge her with distribution?

It was no joke when narcotics officers raided the Junipero Avenue apartment of three California State College at Long Beach students in late March of 1967. They received a tip that the students had been observed rolling a large number of joints there. Officer Ronald E. Dvorak described what happened next: "When we looked in the window, we saw them rolling cigarette paper, inserting a marijuana-like substance in one end and tamping it down with an oriental pipe." More than forty completed joints filled a saucer lying on the kitchen table. "We thought we had the biggest marijuana bust of the year." As the officers entered through an unlocked door and began searching the apartment, one of the three students blurted out, "There's no law against smoking bananas, is there?" She was absolutely correct. "What could we do," Dvorak questioned, "book the kids on suspicion of possession of dangerous bananas?"

A Yale student set up his own banana enterprise and placed a sign near his door that read, "Mellow Yellow Sold Here—Does It Work? Try and See." Up until that point, only three people had made purchases. He noted that one of the side effects of selling banana peel cigarettes was that the remaining pulp was fattening, and commented that he "ate eighteen the first day." His business may have never taken off, but at least he came up with a great slogan: "Tune in, turn on, peel out."

Cambridge banana junkie Jacob Harvot described their hallucinogenic effect. "It is not as high as a marijuana high. But it's quite nice." He added, "You don't just light it like a cigar, of course. The edible part of the banana isn't touched, and you can still slice it on your Wheaties so that Rev. Bob Richards will not be disturbed." (Side note: Richards, who was once referred to as the Vaulting Vicar, is the only male to win the Olympic gold medal in pole vaulting twice, both in 1952 and 1956. He was also the first athlete to appear on a box of Wheaties and their first spokesman.)

An eighteen-year-old Baltimore youth described his Mellow Yellow process: "You have to smoke it steady for about twenty minutes before you get high. It's a slow high." He added that the high feels like "you are viewing the world and you are not there. Like looking through a window."

***

There are far more testimonies on its effectiveness, but one has to question whether these kids really were getting stoned or, instead, experiencing the placebo effect.

Lindsy Van Gelder, reporting for UPI, decided to find out for herself. "We are at a banana party, the newest craze of the psychedelic teenage underground." She described in detail how the banana carver meticulously prepared the banana cigarettes. Once he was done, it was time for her test. She wrote, "I have never smoked anything stronger than a nonfilter cigarette, and I am waiting to fall off my chair in a stupor after the first drag. I puff. Nothing happens. I smoke two banana joints. They taste terrible, and I've gotten higher on root beer." After someone points out that it can take a while for the effect to kick in, she adds, "Three hours later, my mouth tastes awful, but I haven't had even a hint of a high." Van Gelder concluded that the supposed high was "mostly psychological," but her observations clearly lacked any form of scientific rigor.

It was time for the experts to do some real experimentation. Enter the big guns at the United States Food and Drug

Administration (FDA). Commissioner Dr. James L. Goddard stated, "We really don't know what agent, if there is any, in the smoke produces the reported effect but we are investigating to see if it might be the methylated form of serotonin." Otto Heinecke, a regional director for the agency's Bureau of Drug Abuse Control told the press, "We heard about this when it first came up and everybody was laughing about it." He continued, "If we find there is a problem thru [sic] smoking them, we will get together with state and local officials to determine a remedy." Fred Garfield, deputy director of the same bureau, added, "Forbidding the smoking of material from banana peels would require Congressional legislation and I'm confident that such a law would never pass."

One man in Congress was listening when that last statement was made: Frank Thompson, New Jersey's 4th Congressional District representative at the time. (Side note: He was forced to resign on December 29, 1980, after being convicted on bribery and conspiracy charges related to the Abscam scandal.)

According to the Congressional Record, Thompson stood up on April 19, 1967, and addressed the House of Representatives regarding this pressing matter. Thompson spoke at length, so here are just a few of the highlights:

"Mr. Speaker, the US Food and Drug Administration recently launched an investigation into banana peel smoking. This is very good news to me, since I have been extremely concerned over the serious increase in the use of hallucinogenics of youngsters."

"I ask Congress to give thoughtful consideration to legislation entitled, appropriately, the Banana and Other Odd Fruit Disclosure and Reporting Act of 1967. The target is those banana-smoking beatniks who seek a make-believe land, 'the land of Honalee,' as it is described in the peel puffers' secret psychedelic marching song, 'Puff, The Magic Dragon.' "

"Bananas may help explain the trancelike quality of much of the 90th Congress proceedings. Just yesterday I saw on the luncheon menu of the Capitol dining room a breast of chicken Waikiki entry [sic] topped with, of all things, fried bananas."

"Therefore, I propose the Banana Labeling Act of 1967, a bill to require that every banana bear the following stamp, 'Caution: Banana Peel Smoking May Be Injurious to Your Health. Never Put Bananas in the Refrigerator.' " He added, "There is, of course, one practical problem with this legislation: banana peels turn black with age. At that point, the warning sign becomes unreadable."

He concluded, "What we need across the length and breadth of this great land is a grassroots move to ban the banana, to repeal the peel. Howard Johnson's can survive with only twenty-seven flavors. And what is wrong with an avocado split? I will only breathe easier when this country, this land we love, can declare, 'Yes, we have no bananas; we have no bananas today.' "

Clearly, Thompson was having some fun with the topic at hand. The United Fruit Company, which dominated the banana industry in the 1960s, took a far more serious approach to the matter. They called upon Dr. Sidney Cohen, known for his pioneering research on the effects of marijuana, LSD, cocaine, and other mood-altering drugs. He set out to finally prove once and for all whether or not bananas had any effect on the mind.

Cohen's first step was to have his wife Ilse purchase 150 pounds (68 kg) of bananas at their local Safeway Supermarket. Back at their Mandeville Canyon home in Los Angeles, it took Mrs. Cohen and their son Richard three days to scrape together 40 ounces (1.13 kg) of the needed material from all of those banana skins. From that, 50 banana cigarettes were rolled, along with a few dozen made from orange pekoe tea to serve as controls.

Cohen had no problem rounding up volunteers for his experiment. Among non-marijuana users, the results were nearly all unanimous: they either didn't experience any sort of high, or had a mild sense of dizziness. For those that were users, none found the high produced by bananas to be even close to what they experienced with marijuana. In June of 1967, Cohen concluded that smoking bananas was no different than smoking orange pekoe tea (which had previously established non-visionary properties). In other words, both did basically nothing.

As for the FDA results, they completed their testing on May 24, 1967, and stated, "The Bureau of Science has made an analysis of the smoke obtained from several recipes for dried banana and concentrated banana juice" and determined that "there were no detectable quantities of known hallucinogens in these materials." One criticism of their study was that no human subjects were involved. They used a machine that "smoked dried banana peels for more than three weeks and never did get high."

A report published in the *New York State Journal of Medicine* that November found similar results. A study of fifty drug users in Greenwich Village by a New York University medical team concluded that half of those questioned observed either no effects or just subtle effects after smoking bananas. The remaining half experienced some varying effects, including elevation in their mood and hallucinations, and some were made ill. Their conclusion: "The baked skins do produce mild effects on the nervous system, but the main effects seem to be psychological."

If all of this hasn't convinced you that smoking bananas is, well, just plain bananas, there is little else that I can do to stop you. But I do have a suggestion: simply get high on life. There are lots of wonderful things to see and do that don't require the intake of any substance and are far more intoxicating.

Fed a Yak at Midnight

1935

At first glance, one would have seen nothing unusual about sixty-two-year-old Antonio Sclafani as he took his place on the bench in Yorkville Court before Magistrate Adolph Stern on July 2, 1935. He was dressed in a white sport shirt, gray flannel shorts, rolldown silk socks, and white tennis shoes. However, one could not help but notice that he held a basket filled with grapefruit, lettuce, and carrots.

Sclafani had been arrested at midnight in New York City's Central Park Zoo for feeding grapefruit to an omnivorous yak while wearing what Officer Martin Corcoran described as a bathing suit. Corcoran also observed Sclafani feeding lettuce and carrots to zebras.

Dr. Harry Ninphius, zoo veterinarian, had also observed Sclafani feeding the animals and testified that the diet he had chosen for them was not ideal.

Sclafani told the magistrate that he was a nature lover who had a great understanding of animals. He pointed out that everything he fed to the animals was fresh, and he was certain that they enjoyed both his food and his company.

Magistrate Stern concluded that Sclafani did not intend to harm the animals in any way and suspended his sentence.

Love for Lease

1965

The crazy true story of how an elderly millionaire attempted to rent a beautiful, young woman from her husband for a one-year period.

The Isle of Sylt is a beautiful, elongated island located on the northern border between Germany and Denmark. In the 1960s, Sylt became famous for attracting "the rich and the naked"—affluent folks from all around the world wanted to stroll up and down its sandy beaches in the buff. It was in this unusual setting that an American millionaire met the girl of his dreams and had his life changed forever.

William Henry Brown was sixty-one years old, a Princeton graduate, and one of the original financial backers of *Time* magazine. He inherited an estimated ten million dollars (approximately $142 million today) when his father William Harry Brown, a partner in one of the largest coal shippers of the 1800s, died in 1921. With his fortune, the younger Brown had little need to work a full-time job. Instead, he traveled quite a bit between the United States and Europe, owned both a Maserati and a Ferrari, yachted the seas in his mahogany, custom-built *Visitor VI*, fanatically followed the European road racing circuit, and rarely missed a Grand Prix event. While at home in the United States, he would split his time among several locations: El Mirador, his 2,500-acre ranch in Sasabe, Arizona; an apartment in Manhattan; a home in Pittsburgh; and skiing in Aspen, Colorado.

In June of 1963, William Henry Brown met the girl of his dreams—thirty-year-old Beate H. Leber, the daughter of a German private school director. Brown later described their meeting: "She walked on the sand like Venus. She was irresistible. At her left walked a sleek greyhound. One step behind walked a homely man, her husband." That man was Ralph Leber, a German-born writer eleven years her senior.

Immediately smitten, Brown introduced himself to the couple. Since they were all donning their birthday suits at the time, Brown asked if it would be okay to take some photographs of Beate, something he had previously done with twenty-five other women. The regulations at the resort prohibited photography, so the Lebers invited Brown to take pictures at their Heidelberg apartment that Christmas. Shortly after that, a conversation ensued that led to a contract bring drawn up in which Mr. Leber agreed to rent Beate to Brown for a specified fee.

Now that Beate was on lease to Brown, the three traveled together to Switzerland, cruised around the Mediterranean on his yacht for three months, and in March 1964, spent ten days down in the Bahamas aboard the *Visitor IV*.

Invited along for the Bahamas trip was Brown's best friend, sixty-two-year-old Reverend James Holland Beal. He made it clear that he did not approve of Brown's playboy lifestyle, but added, "Frankly, Mr. Leber didn't seem to give a hoot what was going on." He added that Beate and Brown took off in the yacht's dinghy several times, leaving him and Mr. Leber alone on the boat for long periods of time. "Finally I said to the husband, quite bluntly: 'Do you think it is wise to encourage your wife to go off with our host on the boat all day?' He came right back with 'You don't suppose Mr. Brown paid my wife's and my expenses over here from Germany so he could be with me, do you?'" Brown and the Lebers headed back for a stay at El Mirador, after which the Lebers returned to Germany.

There was another trip to the Bahamas that December and additional meetups, as well as a gift of one hundred shares in Time, Inc. worth $6,000 (approximately $49,000 today). But everything began to go south for this three-way relationship in June of 1965, when Beate traveled for the first time to the States without her husband in tow. Beate spent several weeks with Brown and upon returning home to Heidelberg, Ralph Leber finally had enough and threw her out. She ran right into Brown's arms.

In August, the two decided to vacation in Monte Carlo. While there, Beate looked on as Brown was intimate with another woman before heading off to dinner without her. Upon his return, Brown found a penned by Beate that read, "I care for you very much, but my mother complex is stronger. Goodbye."

Beate went back to her husband, and Brown was soon back in Heidelberg begging her forgiveness. This is where contract number two enters the picture.

The "Love for Lease" agreement, which was drawn up by Brown's New York attorney on September 28, 1965, consisted of nine separate clauses. The most significant of these specified that when Beate was to arrive in New York, she was to immediately obtain a divorce with the help of Brown's lawyer. Beate could write to her ex-husband if she wished, but agreed to "gladly give up all verbal, visual and physical contact" with him for a period of six months. Most importantly, Brown agreed to pay Ralph Leber $3,000 per month for a period of one year, "the total with other stipends $39,000." Adjusted for inflation, Brown offered to pay Leber approximately $314,000 to divorce and totally stay away from Beate for six months.

All three signed the contract and on November 1, 1965,
Beate and Brown drove from his ranch to Juarez, Mexico,
where the Lebers were divorced. Immediately after the
proceedings, Brown presented her with what she interpreted
as an engagement ring, but what he later referred to as a
"divorce ring."

For the next six weeks, the two would stay at El Mirador, as
Brown prepared for his annual Christmas party. The December
12, 1965, publication of the *Arizona Daily Star* announced:
"William H. Brown of Sasabe will be host at a party at Tucson
Country Club Saturday. Out of town guests will include
Theodore T. Hayes, who was one of Jack Dempsey's trainers,
and Mrs. Beate Leber of Heidelberg." It was the party at which
Beate was expecting Brown to formally propose to her.

But it was not to happen. Brown discovered a letter that Beate
had written to her ex-husband. In it she said, "Darling, I live
here like a princess. Bill will marry me. He promised to build
me a fairy palace with golden toilet seats. But we must act
cleverly and get as much money out of him as possible."

It was at this point that Brown realized he had been tricked.
The day after the party, he sent Beate packing. Next thing you
know, she filed a $2.5 million (nearly $20 million today) breach
of promise suit against Brown. In return, Brown had charges
filed against Ralph Leber back in Germany. On August 1, 1966,
Leber was found guilty of pandering his wife, sentenced to six
months in jail, and fined 1,000 deutsche marks.

Back in US District Court in Tucson, Arizona, the breach of
promise suit opened on Tuesday, February 21, 1967. Beate was
clearly dressed to impress in a sleeveless A-line dress, matching
leather gloves and shoes, and a tweed jacket. On February
26, *New York Daily News* reporter Jon Kamman wrote, "An

Elizabeth Taylor, Beate is not. But her attraction goes beyond physical appearance." He continued, "The general consensus is that she is a very eye-catching and sexy woman."

As with any disagreement, there are two opposing sides to the story. This was no exception. Beate argued that Brown had promised to marry her several times and that she had written proof of it. Brown, on the other hand, argued that their arrangement was nothing more than that of a man and his mistress.

Beate's lawyer, Raymond Hayes, introduced more than one hundred letters, postcards, and telegrams that Brown had sent to her. Many simply described his interests in yachting, car racing, ranching, and women. He repeatedly made references to how he suffered the effects of gout and a pinched shoulder nerve. But the most incriminating evidence included lines such as "When are you going to marry me?" and "I love you. I want to marry you."

Brown admitted to the court that the two had discussed marriage, but he never made a formal proposal, nor did she ever indicate that she was accepting of such. "At that time I was very much infatuated with the girl. I had thought if circumstances changed—who can tell?" Brown commented, "I was flattered that an old man was getting the attentions of a young girl."

After several days of testimony, the evidence against Brown was quite damaging, and it appeared that Beate's lawyer had built a strong case.

Then, on Friday, February 24, Brown's lawyer, Norman Hull, argued against allowing Beate's Mexican divorce decree to be admitted as evidence. His rationale was that the divorce was based on a contract that was "morally and legally wrong in its conception." Beate's lawyer was shocked by what he heard: Brown had one of his New York lawyers draw up the divorce contract, and now they were arguing that the whole thing was illegal. Judge John C. Bowen ruled in Brown's favor, stating "The divorce was accomplished through illegal means. I don't think any court of law will recognize it as a legal proceeding."

The following Monday, the judge dismissed the entire case on the grounds that, since the Mexican divorce was not legal, the Lebers were still married to one another. Therefore, it was legally impossible for a married woman to wed another man.

After the trial ended, Attorney Hayes told the press, "She is returning to Germany immediately. She will not go back to her husband, Ralph, but probably will enter the import-export business. She will return to the United States when her appeal is heard." He added that Beate had relied upon the advice of Mr. Brown's attorney and that "[t]hey told her she was divorced. She believed them."

Beate never filed that appeal and on July 20, 1967, Hayes stated that she was done filing lawsuits in the United States.

Beate Leber's association with this story would be brought up one more time in the press: when William Henry Brown passed away on November 24, 1972, at the Tucson Medical Center. He was seventy-one years of age.

Husband's Life Is Saved by Wife's Thigh

1939

On April 13, 1939, Mr. and Mrs. George Mackey were awakened by a man who ripped a screen from the window in their apartment. He told them, "I've got you now. You sent my pals to Folsom." He then proceeded to point the gun at Mr. Mackey and said, "You're the guy that sent me up and I'm going to get you for it." Mr. Mackey denied that he had done any such thing, but there is little you can say when you're staring at a loaded gun.

The intruder then said, "Have your wife take off her clothing so I can see her left thigh. If there is a butterfly tattooed there, you're the guy I'm after." Mrs. Mackey did exactly as she was told and disrobed in the dark. The man then shined his flashlight at her thigh and, to the couple's relief, there was no butterfly tattoo.

The intruder then apologized. As he left the premises, he threatened, "I'll find her if I have to search the whole town."

Hee-Haw

1954

Every Christmas, there's that one popular toy that every child must have. Always in short supply, such a gift is so desired by children that parents are willing to pay top dollar to get their hands on one. This is the story of a popular Christmas gift that couldn't fit under the tree. If anything, this unusual gift was more likely to eat the tree.

Have you ever been in the position of needing to purchase a gift for someone, but having absolutely no clue what to get? Let's face it, you don't want just *any* gift. You want the perfect gift. Something that is memorable. Something that is unique.

Well, I have the perfect gift idea for you. It was one of the hottest gifts in the mid-1950s. Elaine Reed had one named Jennie. Jennifer and Jonathan Wise simply adored their Speedy Lopez. One named Pokey belonged to Ricky and Mary Jean Lubrecht. David Campbell owned one named Sancho.

What I am talking about here is a real, live Mexican *burro*. In other words, a donkey.

It's not that burros had never been purchased as pets prior to this. Macy's Department Store sold them in the 1940s, though not in large quantities. No one can say for sure what triggered the burro fad, but most articles trace it back to two different promotions that occurred in the fall of 1954.

The first was when Raymond Dresslar, a manager at Sanger Brothers Department Store in Dallas, walked into his boss' office and asked, "You want to hear a crazy idea?" Soon after,

Dresslar arranged for a little, shaggy, grayish-brown burro named Cisco to be put on display in their toy department. His promotional attraction was a huge success! As Cisco slowly munched away on the hay inside his cedar-log pen, crowds grew larger with each passing day. Cisco was even taken around the city to visit children in hospitals, orphanages, and schools.

Cisco's popularity with the kids soon produced a demand for burros. The first twenty that Sanger acquired sold out quickly, and an additional thirty were ordered. "We sold an even 50 head—two truckloads—at $85 apiece," Dresslar stated. "I tell you we could have sold 200 to 300 more if we had really gone into it commercially."

The second driving force behind the burro craze was Spencer Gifts—the same Spencer Gifts that you find in nearly every mall today—which advertised Mexican burros in their mail-order catalog. They were an instant hit.

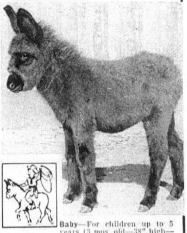

October 1954 Spencer Gifts advertisement for Mexican burros.

It wasn't long before the press picked up on the sudden popularity of burros. Newspaper articles, stories in magazines, and television appearances all helped promote the idea that burros were the perfect pet—make that the perfect Christmas gift. Just like Tickle-Me Elmo, Cabbage Patch dolls, and Beanie

Babies, a Mexican burro was once the must-have Christmas gift that was in short supply.

It wasn't long before others decided to get in on the burro game. While typically sold as Mexican burros, others marketed them as donkeys, Rocky Mountain canaries, mountain canaries, or by the derogatory term "Mexican Jeeps." Whatever the animals were called, promoters claimed that burros were the perfect pet. They were described as docile, good with children, and easy to care for. Most of the burros that were shipped were between four and six months old, and were estimated to reach full size at two years of age. A full-grown adult stood approximately 43 inches (1.1 m) tall and would weigh approximately 200 pounds (91 kg). Clearly, they were not the type of animal that one could keep in an apartment, but they could theoretically be raised in a larger yard or on a farm.

Of course, there were a few drawbacks to owning a burro. First, they could live twenty-five years—well beyond the time needed for their child owners to mature and leave the family nest. They were also known for being a bit slow and for doing things at their own pace. You simply couldn't rush a burro.

Noise production could also be a problem. It was reported on March 23, 1955, that Mr. and Mrs. Walter S. Wright of Idaho had purchased a burro named Milton for their children Kathy and Bruce. Each morning as the sun rose, Milton would bray and wake up the neighbors. After repeated complaints, the Wrights had no choice but to pasture Milton on a ranch outside of the city. One other problem they mentioned was that the children were unable to ride Milton because he was recovering from a back injury. Apparently, another child had whacked Milton with a two-by-four.

In 1954, the typical burro sold for between $65 and $100
(approximately $615 to $950 today). Nearly all were shipped by
freight on board, meaning that the purchaser was responsible
for all shipping costs. The farther one lived from the Mexican
border, the higher the overall cost would be. The majority of
the burros were consigned to the Railway Express Agency for
shipment nationwide. Typically, shipments went smoothly, but
there were times when they didn't. Burros are famous for eating
just about anything, and occasionally they would chow down on
their shipping tags. At 8:54 a.m. on November 29, 1954, a train
pulled into the New Brunswick, New Jersey, train station with a
burro inside one of the cars that had a rope around its neck and
a Railway Express tag attached. It read, "This burro belongs
to New Brunswick, NJ. It ate its destination tag and its record
of attention." After some investigation, it was determined that
the burro was headed to Mrs. Phillip Crockett of Piscataway,
New Jersey. She had purchased the burro to amuse her
grandchildren when they visited.

A short time later, on December 7, history repeated itself in
Cleveland, Ohio. This time, three burros had eaten their tags.
After the railway company contacted the shipper in Laredo,
Texas, it was determined that one was headed to Lexington,
Kentucky, another to North Jackson, Ohio, and the last to
Oyster Bay, New York.

Yet none received more attention than Judy the Burro, who
arrived at the Railway Express office in Rochester, New York,
on May 1, 1955. Her tag had been consumed by a second
burro that was traveling along with her. A claim for Judy was
put in by 5-year-old Pamela Joan Mottes of Stafford Springs,
Connecticut, but she was surely disappointed when Max
Spencer Adler, founder of Spencer Gifts, stated that the burro
she ordered for her birthday was most likely still in transit.

Donald C. Waite of Oakland, California, thought that Judy may be the prize he'd been awarded in a New York toy firm's contest. There was also a Fairmont, Minnesota, man who claimed that a burro he ordered had never arrived, and said that perhaps Judy was his. On May 9, the mystery of Judy's destination was finally solved when she received her tag. Her true owner was Eldon D. Henderson of Sandusky, Michigan.

But the wayward donkey problem continued. Three days later, it was reported that a goat named Lena and a Mexican burro named Bessie had arrived at the Railway Express office in Detroit, both lacking tags. What's interesting is that, just like Judy, Bessie had been shipped from Rochester, New York, to her new owner located in Sandusky. What are the chances that two different burros would be shipped from Rochester to Sandusky at the same time? Could Judy and Bessie have possibly been the same burro? From that point on, Railway Express workers were instructed to tie the shipping tags to each animal's tail.

Which begs the question: who was supplying all of these burros? Various articles point to three men.

The Sanger Brothers Department Store purchased their burros from J. W. Cranford of Corsicana, Texas, but little else is known about his operation.

Dr. Antonio Cavazos sold over two thousand burros annually and operated facilities on both sides of the border: in Laredo, Texas, and Nuevo Laredo, Mexico. When interviewed in 1954, he said that he had been raising and importing burros for fifty years. Some were sold as pack animals, some for donkey baseball, and others as pets.

Then there was veterinarian Dr. Fred Schmidt, owner of the Poverty Flat Ranch near Douglas, Arizona. When interviewed on March 31, 1956, he stated, "The burros were roaming the area wild. The border is nearby, and the burros were easily imported. Even eighteen years ago, eastern folk wanted the animals so I started selling them. But my business was nothing like it is today."

With the sudden explosion in demand for burros, the Mexican government placed an embargo on them. Dr. Schmidt anticipated that this would happen, so he arranged to import a large number of females. At the time of the interview, he had 250 in his breeding stock. "I get my relaxation from my burros. All my spare time goes into those critters. I enjoy it and every time I send out another carload shipment I know that a lot of youngsters will be made happy. That's relaxation enough for me."

Sadly, Doc Schmidt suffered a heart attack and passed away nine days later, at forty-five-years of age. He and a roping partner had won first place in a team-tying contest the previous night, and on the day of his death they fought a grass fire. His herd of burros was sold off, with sixty of them being purchased by Robert A. Phillips to raise on his Shetland pony ranch in Ocala, Florida.

The passing of Dr. Schmidt coincided with a sharp decline in the demand for burros. Like any fad, this one had run its course. Soon there were far more classified ads for people wishing to sell their burros than there were of retailers promoting them.

So if you are considering purchasing a burro this coming Christmas, you should probably order early. They could be in short supply if they suddenly become popular again.

Jerry the Mule Facing Execution

1936

On June 22, 1936, it was announced in the press that Jerry, a thirty-year-old mule at the Olive View Sanatorium in Sylmar, California, had been declared unfit for further work. As a result, an application had been filed with the Board of Supervisors to put Jerry down.

Mrs. Grace Gossard, assistant to the sanatorium superintendent, stated, "I feel sorry for Jerry and while a last-minute reprieve might be granted, Jerry's infirmity probably will be ended by a quick, painless death. Jerry has reached the stage where he has to sleep standing up. If he ever lay down he never could get up again. His teeth are gone, too."

Jerry had been retired to a hog ranch at the sanatorium several months prior, but the first thing he did upon arrival was attack a 1,600-pound (726 kg) Clydesdale horse.

The county supervisor offered to allow Jerry to live on his Glendale farm for the remainder of his life. On July 13, 1936, Jerry was put up for sale at a county auction. Since county officials were barred from bidding on county property, the Anti-Vivisection Society stepped in and purchased Jerry for $1. The organization then turned Jerry over to the county supervisor, so that the mule could enjoy his retirement.

The Shoe Bandit

1956

Just what would make someone want to steal another person's shoes?

The city of Coronado sits directly across the bay from San Diego, California. It is home to a naval base, beach resorts, and the community that lives there. No one took much notice when a seemingly petty and insignificant crime took place there on September 13, 1956. It was a Thursday evening when someone climbed a ladder and broke into the second-floor apartment of Lieutenant and Mrs. M. A. Katz at 401 D Avenue. The thief stole three pairs of shoes and a wallet containing about $11.00 ($100 today).

Two days later, people began to take notice when a house about six blocks away experienced a similar crime. This time, in broad daylight, someone entered the 249 Palm Avenue home of Mrs. Nathan T. Howell, walking off with twenty pairs of her size 5½ shoes.

Was this the work of one person? Could this have been a bunch of kids clowning around? Possibly even a copycat crime? No one could say for sure.

Then, something odd began to occur. Single shoes started popping up all over town. Within one week of the crimes first being reported, two of Mrs. Katz's and nine of Mrs. Howell's shoes were found. There seemed to be no rhyme or reason as to where they were dropped—in a garden, on a football field, or in a vacant lot. While no fingerprints were found on any of the shoes, two unusual observations were made: no two shoes made a pair, and nearly all of those found were left-footed.

Very strange.

On September 27, the Coronado police got their first big break in the case. Fifteen-year-old Gary N. Bunker was delivering a newspaper to 714 F Avenue around 5:00 in the evening and as he went on his route, he saw a man jump from a lower window and run down the street. Police discovered four pairs of shoes belonging to Mrs. Barry C. Taylor wrapped in one of her brown skirts just inside the window through which the burglar had escaped. Investigators concluded that when Bunker tossed his paper on the doorstep, the thief likely became frightened, dropped his loot, and made a run for it.

The newsboy described the suspect as being a white male, twenty-five to thirty years in age, 5 foot 9 inches (175 cm) tall, 190 pounds (86 kg), and stocky in build, with light brown hair in a butch cut. With a military base located on the peninsula, there were quite a few men who matched this description.

On Thursday, October 4, the shoe burglar struck the home of Mr. and Mrs. Henry F. Kramp on 1310 7th Street and took three pairs of her shoes, a few articles of clothing, and her purse. Two pairs were recovered about eight blocks away the following day. This was followed up by a similar heist of clothing, a purse, and five pairs of shoes from the 151 F Avenue residence of Colonel and Mrs. J. P. Tredwell.

A total of five shoe robberies occurred within a six-week period, and all happened within a short distance of one another. Coronado residents surely had a serial shoe bandit on their hands. Up to that point, no one was harmed during the robberies. This would all change on Sunday, October 28, 1956.

For some strange reason, on that day the thief returned to the scene of his second offense: the Howell home. As he entered the house's garage from the rear, he noticed a bowling pin lying in a pile of kindling. He picked it up and headed toward Mrs. Howell's closet. While he was loading up his bounty, Mrs. Howell suddenly walked into the room. He struck Mrs. Howell over the head with the bowling pin, forcibly grabbed her, and placed his hand over her mouth. Mrs. Howell instinctively bit down as hard as she could and managed to break free. She ran out of the house screaming as neighbors came to her rescue. It took eleven stitches to close the gash on her head, and the burglar made off with sixteen pairs of her shoes, some of which had been recovered from the first robbery.

The *Coronado Journal* questioned Police Chief Robert H. Manchester on his department's progress in capturing the shoe bandit. He assured the public that his men were doing everything possible, but he was not willing to reveal specific details of the investigation. He stated, "Naturally, I know that neither you nor any of the interested citizens would want or expect a full public exposure of the action we are taking, as this would only serve to minimize our efforts." He added, "One interesting point in the case is that, while numerous shoes, identified as having been stolen locally, have been recovered, we have also recovered many other shoes which cannot be identified by local residents and which we must assume have been stolen from homes in other communities."

On February 20, 1957, it was reported that four women in San Diego had been attacked. Each told a similar story: a man dressed in pajamas leapt out from the bushes, knocked them to the ground, and ran off with one of their shoes, almost always the left one.

Had the shoe thief given up on Coronado and moved on to San Diego? No. One week later, four pairs of shoes were stolen in Coronado. Over the next year, there were sporadic reports of shoes being stolen in both localities. Interestingly, all of the robberies in San Diego were of the knockdown-and-steal-one variety, while those in Coronado always involved the theft of multiple pairs at the same time.

On the evening of May 8, 1958, twenty-year-old divorcee Betty Garlitz was watching television in her Coronado home with twenty-five-year-old Navy Lieutenant (j.g.) Arthur F. Vohden. After having noticed an intruder sneak in through a door that was slightly ajar, Vohden jumped up out of his seat, gave chase, and captured the man.

(Side note: Vohden was in training to be an astronaut and had made national headlines two weeks earlier as the first man to spend twenty-four hours in space. He later married Lavell E. Kohring on September 17, 1960. After a short illness, twenty-nine-year-old Vohden passed away on November 18, 1961. His daughter was born ten days later.)

Police identified the suspect as twenty-three-year-old Navy Lieutenant (j.g.) Wayne Snow McFarland of Houston, Texas. Vohden and McFarland were both pilots stationed at the naval airbase in Coronado. Betty Garlitz told police that McFarland had previously visited her home and was aware that she lived there alone with her two-and-a-half-year-old daughter. What he didn't expect upon his sneaky return was that Vohden would be present and bring an end to his crime spree.

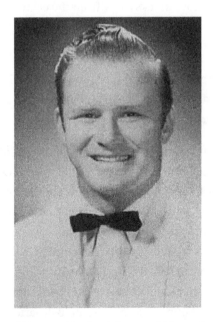

1955 University of Houston Yearbook image of Wayne Snow McFarland.

McFarland readily admitted that he was the shoe bandit. He stated, "I can give no reason why I did these things—I wish I knew." Police found a number of the snatched shoes both in his apartment and hidden under two homes. His bail was set at $20,000 ($175,000 today) on the single charge of assault with a deadly weapon—in his case, assault with a deadly bowling pin.

The front page of the May 15, 1958, *Coronado Journal* featured a large photograph of two shoes. The first belonged to a seventeen-year-old Houston, Texas, girl who had been raped on December 27, 1957. The second shoe was recovered from McFarland's Coronado apartment. Both shoes were described as "blue, spike heeled pumps, size 6B, with same brand and serial number, 6B4123." It had been determined that Wayne McFarland was four blocks away from the crime scene on that date.

Ultimately, McFarland was charged with fifteen counts of burglary, robbery, attempted rape, and assault. His attorney, Percy Foreman, planned to have McFarland plead not guilty by reason of insanity.

At a preliminary hearing during the second week of June, victims identified McFarland as the shoe bandit. One woman described how he had knocked her down while she was walking home from a bus stop. Another testified that he had entered her home and proceeded to beat and choke her as she tried to scream. Perhaps most damaging, however, was the testimony of Mrs. Dorothy Howell, the woman he hit with the bowling pin. She stated that she had been hit so hard that "it knocked [her] out of [her] pumps" and went on to describe the entire horrific event.

On August 30, McFarland opted to plead guilty to the charges, but the judge suspended all further court proceedings until psychiatric examinations were completed. Then on November 6, doctors at Atascadero State Hospital reported that they determined McFarland to be a sexual psychopath.

In January of 1959, a plumber was doing some work in one of the officers' barracks at the North Island Naval Air Station. Beneath the floorboards, he discovered two bags containing 133 additional shoes and an assortment of women's undergarments and clothing.

March 17, 1960, would be judgement day for McFarland. His parents begged the court for leniency. The doctors at Atascadero explained that they had successfully treated McFarland and he was no longer a threat to the public. Their suggestion was probation, but Judge Clarence Harden was unconvinced. Arguing that "Probation would be shocking to the community," he handed down a prison sentence of ten years to life.

After Wayne Snow McFarland was released from prison, he wed Judith Ann Wurzell on August 23, 1969. The marriage would end in divorce on September 12, 1994. He was sixty-four years old when he passed away on February 24, 1999, in Port Arthur, Texas.

Educated Women Are Unfit as Wives

1904

Since the beginning of time, people have made outrageous claims with little to no proof of their truth. Take, for example, these ludicrous assertions that Dr. A. Lathrone Smith of Bishop's College, Montréal, and Vermont University at Burlington made during an address to the American Medical Association on June 7, 1904. His message warned against what he called "the barbarous practice of over-educating our girls."

He claimed, "Higher education unfits girls for motherhood. The mental strain affects the nerves and makes them dread matrimony more than did the girls of another generation, because they realize that their physical systems are weaker and less able to endure the strain and responsibility of motherhood."

Dr. Smith offered what he considered a simple and effective plan to prevent young women from succumbing to an overdose of intellect. "Cut out Greek, Latin, mythology, and algebra, and turn them [young women] out of school at an earlier age. Give the girls an opportunity to rest after a schooling that is practical and useful, and let them build up their physical systems for the trials of wifehood. Youthful love founds a stronger home and produces more healthy children. Young married couples who are not overeducated have the healthiest children."

He continued, "Over study in school, then more study in music, painting and perhaps something else, stunts the girl physically. Although it may improve her intellect, it ruins her for motherhood."

The Womanless Library

1930

During the Great Depression, Le Mars, Iowa, was front-page news for three seemingly unrelated stories, all tied together by an incredibly misogynistic bequest made by one of its prominent attorneys.

I have done quite a bit of reflecting as I approach the end of my teaching career. And looking back, it is clear to me that nearly everything that I am today is due to the positive influence that women have had on me. Those include my mother Eileen, my wife Mary Jane, and my friends, colleagues, and students. It's difficult to express in words the incredible respect that I have for women, which makes the story that you are about to read all the more disturbing to me. It's the story of a man who outwardly seemed to adore women while he was alive, but revealed his true disdain for them shortly after he died.

The beginning of this bizarre story can be traced back to the crisis that plagued rural farmers of the midwestern United

States in the years following World War I. Until this point, farmers enjoyed ever-growing production and profits. This required them to purchase more acreage and equipment, and caused them to take on additional debt. As is the case with most financial bubbles, the farmers were headed for a crash, and were ultimately hit with a triple whammy. To run their farms efficiently, expensive machinery was required. This mechanization caused overproduction, which, in turn, led to sudden price deflation.

While industries could simply lay off workers and idle manufacturing plants, farmers lacked a similar option. Farm employees were typically family members, not hired hands. Food was still needed to care for their livestock, and idle land produced no income to pay off the hefty farm loans.

Perhaps no other family better portrayed this farming crisis than that of Edward Durband Sr. of Struble, Iowa. He first gained great wealth as a savvy businessman, and built on it by buying and selling farmland.

In 1919, Durband, with partner William Nicholson, landed one of the county's largest land deals at the time and purchased 1,600 acres for $600,000 ($8.8 million today). Durband then turned around and tried to sell about 620 acres of the land, but the deal collapsed. For legal representation, he turned to attorney Townsend Murphy "T. M." Zink from nearby Le Mars, Iowa. Zink would be the link that tied three seemingly unrelated stories together.

Durband, with Zink representing him, lost the case. On appeal, he was awarded $34,382.80 (about $532,600 today) plus interest—far less than what he owed on the mortgage. As a result, Durband lost the land in 1924.

Desperate for money, Durband mortgaged 480 acres of his 640-acre farm, but soon lost it all. The last 160 acres, which included the family home, were placed into receivership and sold in a sheriff's sale on the Le Mars courthouse steps. The buyer? None other than lawyer T. M. Zink. Durband now had to pay Zink rent to continue the operation of his farm.

In addition to the ongoing farm crisis, the prohibition of alcohol was a major issue in the 1920s. One of Le Mars's strongest supporters of prohibition was Maybelle Knox, president of the Plymouth County chapter of the Woman's Christian Temperance Union.

At 9:30 p.m. on Saturday, June 8, 1929, Knox was standing outside Joe Duster's soft drink parlor at 22 Central Avenue SE in Le Mars and overheard one of his customers state, "Let's go in and get a drink." She immediately went to the mayor's office and shortly thereafter, the suspected speakeasy was raided. No "likker" was found, but Knox stood by her claim that there had been plenty of alcohol on the premises. In turn, Duster retained the services of T. M. Zink's law firm, Kass, Zink & Kass, and filed a $15,000 ($223,000 today) suit against Knox in June of 1929.

Zink would never get to represent Joe Duster in court. On Thursday, September 4, 1930, Zink was rushed to the Sacred Heart hospital in Le Mars. The diagnosis was gallstones, and doctors concluded that surgery was required—a risky and dangerous procedure in the 1930s. At first, his condition was reported to have been satisfactory. But Zink took a turn for the worse and passed away on September 11, 1930, at seventy-two years of age.

For a time, the citizens of Le Mars turned their attention away from the farmers' hardships and the legal troubles of Maybelle Knox. The death of T. M. Zink soon made headlines worldwide.

As with many prominent community members, the news of his passing was initially limited to newspapers in Le Mars and its surrounding area. The September 15th publication of the *Le Mars Globe-Post* stated that, "In the passing of Mr. Zink, this city and the members of the bar of this community, lose a real, honest man of high standing and ideas." An editorial in that same day's paper said, "If T. M. Zink had been able to attend his own funeral, he would have been touched by the evidences of affection and esteem which his fellowmen have held him." The author continued, "there were many who sensed in a greater or less degree his underlying goodness; many to whom he had been kind in his unobtrusive way; many who had cause to see his passing with regret."

The *Le Mars Semi-Weekly Sentinel* wrote: "His name is one that will last as long as the history of Le Mars secures a place in any record of moment." If only they had the foresight to know just how true those words would become. Within forty-eight hours of that statement being set down in ink, the contents of Zink's will would be revealed, and the eyes of the world would be focused on Le Mars.

A document drawn up on July 18, 1930—less than two months before his death—began, "I, T. M. Zink of Le Mars, Iowa, being of sound mind and memory hereby make, publish and declare this to be my last will and testament, hereby expressly and unreservedly revoking any and all wills heretofore made by me."

Things got interesting at the fourth paragraph: "Pay to my daughter, Margretta T. Becker, the sum of five dollars, provided she shall survive me." Adjusted for inflation, he left his daughter a whopping $76.

In the next paragraph, he stated, "I make no provision for my wife, Ida Bennison Zink, owing to the prenuptial contract between us, which will be found with this will...." If she wanted to continue living in their house, he added, "she shall have the option to rent it for forty dollars per month for such time as she wishes." That would be approximately $610 per month today.

As for the remainder of his estate, he requested that it be placed into a trust to be managed by the Le Mars Loan and Trust for a period of seventy-five years, or for "as long as the government of the United States shall exist, and thereafter until destroyed by revolution, or other cause...."

The money was to be lent out in the form of first farm mortgages, or invested in United States bonds. Certainly not the greatest vehicles for yielding investments, these options were relatively stable and secure in the 1920s.

It was estimated that, at the time of his death, Zink was worth somewhere between $40,000 and $80,000. Let that mature for seventy-five years while gaining 4 percent per year, and that value inflates to between $750,000 and $1.5 million. At 6 percent per year, his estate would grow to be between $1.5 and $3 million dollars.

At the end of the seventy-five-year period, he asked that no more than 25 percent of the estate be used to purchase a site where a non-circulating library would be built. An additional 25 percent would be "invested in the best, most reliable and authentic books, maps, charts, works of art, magazines, and other authentic works containing all known information and knowledge of science, literature, geography, religions, and all known knowledge of the world."

The document continued, "No book, work of art, map, or chart shall be excluded therefrom on account of any theory, philosophy, ethics, religion, or language; it being my intention and purpose to establish a library in which all known human knowledge may be found by any man wishing the same."

He stated later in his will that the library would be available to all of those "over fifteen years of age, regardless of religious faith, political affiliation, color, race or nationality, or place of residence, except to alien enemies of the United States of America."

While this all makes him seem like quite the forward thinker, particularly for 1930, he did note one big exception. It was a whopper that instantly brought Zink worldwide fame.

He insisted on the following exclusion to his proposed library: "No woman shall at any time, under any pretense or for any purpose be allowed inside the library, or upon the premises, or have any say about anything concerned therewith, nor appoint any person or persons to perform any act connected therewith. No book, work of art, chart, magazine, picture, unless some production by a man, shall be allowed inside or outside the building."

And just in case he didn't make it clear enough that women could not be involved with this library in any way, he added, "There shall be over each entrance to the premises and building a sign in these words: 'No Woman Admitted'." He continued, "It is my intention to forever exclude all women from the premises and having anything to say or do with the trust estate and library."

Zink's will further explained, "My intense hatred of women is not of recent origin, or development, nor based upon any personal differences I ever had with them, but is the result of my experiences with women, observations of them, and study of all literatures and philosophical works, within my limited knowledge, related thereto."

Ida told the press that her husband was "most gracious to [women] socially," but found them to be difficult to deal with in a professional setting.

Ouch! All of this coming from a man who was at his first wife's bedside when she passed away and had recently remarried.

Zink was specific as to how his estate should be handled. So as to not bore you with the details—his will was ten typewritten pages in length—here is a quick overview: The building and the land that the library was to be built upon would be chosen by a group of three men over the age of fifty. The specific contents of the library would be chosen by three additional men, all over the age of forty. None of these six men could be affiliated with any religious organization. And, should the library never be built, then the trust would become an endowment for the State University law library.

Le Mars city officials had a big dilemma on their hands. If they accepted the terms of Zink's bequest, the town would forever be a tourist attraction. People would come from all around to see the world's only womanless library. Yet at the same time, it wasn't politically prudent for any community to have a womanless library.

On October 14, 1930, the lawyer representing Margretta, Zink's forty-two-year-old daughter from his first marriage, filed paperwork in the district court that questioned the validity of the will. There were nine claims made, beginning with the accusation that Zink "was of unsound mind and not capable of making such will," and concluding with the suggestion that the document was "an insult to American womanhood and of the world. [It] would constitute a libel and a slander, and is contrary to public morals."

There was talk in the press that a settlement might be reached between Margretta and the administrators of the estate, but that agreement never materialized. There was also talk that the state's attorney general was gearing up for a possible fight, but that didn't happen either.

Instead, when the case made it to court the following March, few witnesses testified. Only one had a major impact on the case: Dr. George Donahoe from the state mental hospital in Cherokee. He examined letters penned by Zink and concluded that "Mr. Zink was suffering from a classic case of sexual paranoia, which is a form of insanity that is chronic, progressive and incurable."

He continued, "His obsession was on the female sex. He displaced the ordinary conception of God with a female creatress who is malicious, capricious, and thoroughly unreliable. She has created men for her own amusement, and invented women for the same reason she invented diseases, wars, calamities, for the sole purpose of tormenting men, which gives her pleasure. But for all the creatress' inventions for the harrying of men the most efficient is women."

None of the attorneys representing the city of La Mars, the county, or the state challenged Dr. Donahoe's claims. And with that, on March 7, 1931, Judge C. W. Pitts handed down his ruling: "It is hereby ordered, adjudged determined and decreed that the said T. M. Zink died intestate and that the contestant herein to wit Margretta T. Becker, is the sole and only heir at law of said T. M. Zink, deceased."

The decision brought an abrupt end to the Zink womanless library. It never came to be. His daughter inherited everything, although it had been revealed in court that the value of the estate had dropped significantly since the Great Depression hit. At best, Zink's holdings were worth $25,000, but the deepening worldwide economic crisis and an ever-growing legal bill reduced this by an even greater amount. By the end of the year, the value of the estate had dropped precipitously to about $10,000.

***

On Monday, April 20, 1931, six weeks after the Zink estate ruling, the jury would finally be seated in the case of Joe Duster vs. Maybelle Knox. Opening statements were made, a few witnesses were called to the stand, and later in the day, the two sides reached a settlement.

Duster agreed to withdraw his lawsuit if Knox made a public announcement that no alcoholic beverages were found at his parlor, and that the statements she had made against the establishment were unjustified.

Knox suddenly became suspiciously ill and was not present in court at the time of the judge's announcement. Her husband Sumner sat with her attorney as the following statement was read in the courtroom: "It is undisputed that on the occasion of the alleged search of Joe Duster's soft drink parlor on June 8, 1929, no intoxicating liquors were found, nor was there anything discovered that would tend to show that Duster had been engaged in the illegal sale of intoxicating liquor at that place." Both sides agreed to split the court expenses.

With Knox's case now settled, Le Mars could once again focus its attention on the legal challenges being brought against the Zink estate.

On Thursday, July 2, 1931, Zink's widow Ida filed a claim for $2,929.83. Mrs. Zink alleged that, since June of 1925, she had paid all of the household expenses, including the electric bill, groceries, and restaurant checks. Regarding the prenuptial agreement that she had agreed to at the time of their marriage on February 28, 1925, a visitor to the court commented that "[a]ny man who can get his wife to sign such a contract and who can get her to pay his living expenses, may be adjudged crazy by the court, but he ain't so bad just the same. He's crazy like a fox."

Perhaps the most significant challenge to the estate was a promissory note for $10,000 ($152,000 today) that had been filed two days after Zink's death. It was originally received by a Le Mars bank in an envelope postmarked Kansas City. The note, signed by Mr. Zink in April of 1930, was payable to a woman named Irene Brown. Since the document had not been sworn and affirmed, bank officials questioned its validity. If the document proved to be legitimate, payment would have effectively wiped out every single dollar remaining in Zink's estate. Correspondence between the bank and Ms. Brown's attorneys in Sioux Falls commenced, but no resolution was achieved between the two parties. A suit was then filed on Ms. Brown's behalf with the court, but quickly withdrawn.

After news of the promissory note broke in late December of 1931, reporters in Le Mars, Des Moines, and Sioux City jumped on the story. None could locate Ms. Brown—she seemed to have vanished off of the face of the Earth. With such a large portion of her inheritance at risk, Margretta Becker sought the help of professionals. She hired the Burns Detective Agency in New York.

Investigators obtained their first clue to solving this mystery in Laurel, Nebraska. They learned that a woman named Maybelle Trow Knox—the same Maybelle Knox who raided Joe Duster's soft drink parlor—owned farmland in that area and had been unable to pay her mortgage. To avoid losing the property, she provided the mortgage holder, Union Central Life Insurance, with a promissory note for $2,500. That note had been supplied by the mysterious Irene Brown, and then endorsed over to Union Central by Mrs. Knox. And just where was Irene Brown going to get all that money from? She insinuated that she would soon be receiving a large payout from the estate of T. M. Zink.

Detectives soon learned that Irene Brown had occasionally lodged at the Cataract Hotel in Sioux Falls, South Dakota, and that she looked very similar to Mrs. Knox—so similar that they could pass for twins. After further investigation, detectives determined that the two women were, in fact, the same person. Knox invented the Irene Brown persona in an attempt to fraudulently obtain money from the Zink estate.

On March 10, 1932, a Plymouth County grand jury handed down an indictment against Knox, charging her with forgery of a legal document. Knox insisted that she was innocent and that the real Irene Brown, whom she described as being quiet and shy, would soon step forward to exonerate her.

Less than two weeks later, Knox and her husband were arrested in Kansas City after attempting to hire a woman to impersonate Irene Brown. Their plan was simple: A woman would come forward and testify that she had met T. M. Zink in a hotel café, they became friends, and she had loaned him $10,000. After the existence of Irene Brown had been proven, Knox planned to file a $50,000 lawsuit against the Zink estate for malicious prosecution. A portion of that monetary award would have been used to pay off the impersonator they hired. They failed to realize that one of the women they asked to do the job was married to a federal postal inspector. Oops...

Her bondsman, Morris Levich of Sioux City, immediately withdrew his bond. Knox was brought back home and locked in the county jail.

Her trial for the forged document opened on Monday, May 22, 1932. Knox claimed to be too weak to walk into the courtroom and asked to be carried in. Then, just as the jury was seated, she dramatically fainted and had to be taken home. She was still in a "coma" the next morning and was ordered to seek treatment in the hospital. On December 9, Knox finally admitted that she had forged the promissory note and pleaded guilty to the charge of forgery. She was sentenced to one year in prison at the state penitentiary in Fort Madison.

While that $10,000 promissory note proved to be fraudulent, this would not be the end of the trouble related to the Zink estate. Ed Durband died on November 20, 1932, and farm operations fell into the hands of Ed Jr., his son. With the prices of meat, milk, and produce plummeting, the younger Durband was unable to pay his annual rent to Zink's daughter Margretta and her husband Clarence. The Beckers secured a new tenant, and the Durbands were informed that they had to leave.

Everything seemed quiet until April 17—the day the Durbands were expected to vacate the farm. Word had spread that Sherriff F. E. Rippey was on his way to carry out the eviction order. Instead, hundreds of farmers gathered at the farm and threatened to "shoot it out" should the Durbands be forced to leave. For days, the farmers worked in shifts guarding the Durband farm. Wives brought meals as their husbands made it clear that the Durbands were staying put.

Everything reached a climax on April 27. A group of farmers went to the Becker home and demanded that they allow the Durbands to remain on the farm, but Clarence refused to give in.

An estimated one hundred angry farmers then stormed into the Le Mars courtroom of fifty-three-year-old District Court Judge Charles C. Bradley. He immediately said, "This is my courtroom. Take off your hats and stop smoking cigarettes."

A group of men lunged forward and grabbed the judge by his throat and legs. They demanded that he not sign additional foreclosure actions. As they issued their demands, Bradley's face was punched and slapped, but still he refused to make any promises. The mob then dragged the judge through the courtroom, down the hallway, and down the steps outside. Once again, they repeated their demands, but the judge once again refused.

Another group of men then loaded Judge Bradley into a truck and drove out of town, as others followed behind in their vehicles. They stopped when the group reached a crossroads about 1.5 miles (2.4 km) south of Le Mars. The judge was pulled out of the vehicle and the crowd once again stated their demands. The men resumed their physical attacks, but the judge refused to give in.

"Taken from the truck, I was blindfolded from behind by someone I did not recognize," Judge Bradley later stated. "Someone threw grease from a hubcap on my hair and also tossed sand in my face and hair."

Suddenly, someone pulled out a thick rope and tied a noose around his neck. As the crowd lifted Bradley up by the rope, he suddenly passed out and was allowed to fall back down to the ground. About one minute later he regained consciousness and said a prayer for the down-and-out farmers, but still refused to agree to their demands.

Calls were once again made to hang the judge and he was dragged to a nearby telephone pole. The rope was thrown up over a sign attached to the pole and tightened by the ringleaders. The crowd argued whether it was better to hang the judge or to tie him to a car and drive away with him dragging behind.

"While I was praying someone kept a continual tugging on the rope. Then my prayer finished, someone took my trousers down and threw grease and sand in my trousers. There were some threats of mutilation."

Badly beaten, Judge Bradley stood up and started the long walk back to Le Mars. Farmers offered him a ride, but he turned them down. He later accepted a lift from a man who didn't witness the crime.

Le Mars was once again thrown into the national spotlight. The next day, Governor Herring issued a statement calling the attack "a vicious and criminal conspiracy and assault upon a judge while in discharge of his official duties, endangering his life and threatening a complete breakdown of law and order." He declared martial law for the entire county and called in four national guard companies.

Even with a military presence, H. R. Schultz—who was both the co-executor of T. M. Zink's estate and co-administrator of the farm from which the Durbands were being evicted— reported that a brick had been thrown through a window of his home. Attached was a note that said, "If the Durband brothers are forced to leave their farm, you and Becker will be shot on sight." A few days later, on May 2, the family opted to peacefully vacate the farm.

It was reported on May 7 that 125 suspects had been arrested since martial law had been declared. Famed lawyer Clarence Darrow, who was seventy-six years of age at the time, offered to defend the arrested farmers.

On May 10, 1933, twelve days after it he sent the troops in, Governor Herring declared an end to martial law.

Reports in the press suggest that nearly all of those arrested were released and/or given a small fine for their actions. Seven men were tried for their direct involvement in the attempted lynching of Judge Bradley, and they received sentences ranging from one to six months in duration. Clarence Darrow did not take part in the defense of any of those men.

Ultimately, on August 29, 1933, the court ruled against the Durbands and stated that they were to pay all damages in full to the Zink estate. Since the family had no money, their corn crop was used to pay what was owed. Ten days later, the Durband family declared bankruptcy.

On May 12, 1937, the body of T. M. Zink was disinterred from the cemetery in Le Mars. He was reburied next to the grave of his first wife in Manchester, Iowa. Zink's second wife Ida passed away in her apartment at Le Mars's Union Hotel on October 7, 1940.

His daughter Margretta went on to live a long life. She died in April of 1979 at ninety-two years of age. It's nearly impossible to determine how much she inherited after all the dust had finally settled. Surprisingly, much of this litigation could have been avoided. On January 9, 1935, it was announced that a notarized deed dated August 25, 1920 had been rediscovered. In it, Zink had conveyed all his property, both real and personal, to his daughter. It had all been Margretta's the entire time.

The title of a May 4, 1933, article in the *Carroll Daily Herald* summarized all of what had happened in one single sentence: "Le Mars Residents Begin to Think Zink Estate, With Its Queer Will, Has Operated As Jinx to Locality."

Believe it or not, there's still one more final chapter to this Le Mars story, but it had little to do with the Zink estate. It did, however, involve Maybelle Knox. The story continues in "The Search for Lucinda Trow."

PART 4

HOAXES
& CON ARTISTS

The Search for Lucinda Trow

1938

Maybelle Knox was the center of perhaps the greatest mystery to ever occur in Le Mars. A story so fantastic, it captured the attention of an entire nation.

The last we heard from Maybelle Knox, she was serving time for submitting a fraudulent claim against the Zink estate. Upon her release, Knox did her best to stay out of trouble. Turns out that was something she wasn't very good at.

In November of 1938, rumors began to spread around town that Knox's mother, eighty-year-old Lucinda Trow, had not been seen in quite some time. In her later years, Lucinda rarely ever left her home as her late husband's $90 per month (approximately $1,600 today) Civil War Veteran's pension paid her expenses. She was often seen sitting on her back porch or in front of a window, but that had since ceased.

On Monday, November 7, 1938, two reporters from the *Le Mars Globe-Post* decided to visit Mrs. Trow's home to investigate. Can you guess who answered the door? If you guessed that it was her daughter Maybelle, you'd be correct. Due to a lack of income, she had been forced to take up residence in her mother's home.

Knox told the reporters that she didn't allow anyone to see her mother because it caused her to become agitated, which ultimately meant a sleepless night for the both of them. The reporters explained that they needed to interview her mom to confirm that she was okay. Knox agreed and the reporters returned at 3:00 p.m. to interview Mrs. Trow.

When they arrived, there was no one home. Since Knox had a history of fainting spells—remember her supposed coma during her trial?—reporters were afraid that she may have had a heart attack. The matter was reported to the police. Permission to enter the premises was given by the Le Mars city council two days later, but the home was found to be empty. Later that day, a local constable went over to padlock the house and was surprised to find Knox at home.

On Thursday the 10th, the *Le Mars Globe-Post* received a tip that Knox's dog was lying dead in her backyard. The reporters did not find the Pekingese, but were approached by her neighbor Charles Bingenheimer. He informed the reporters that Knox had taken her mom to Nebraska to celebrate Thanksgiving with relatives. She had asked him to keep a watch on the house while she was gone. He agreed and she lent him a key. Fearing that the dog may be sick or dying inside, Mr. Bingenheimer agreed to allow the reporters into the house. Upon entering, they were immediately confronted by the sounds of a woman moaning in distress. They went up to Lucinda Trow's bedroom and found Knox lying on the bed in great pain and nearly passed out. She declined the help of a doctor, but was willing to accept the ultimate cure for everything: orange sherbet.

Knox explained why she broke off the interview on Monday afternoon. "My mother has changed so much in recent years I was afraid people wouldn't believe that she was the same woman. I thought it best to take her to Nebraska where she wouldn't be annoyed."

Knox said that the two had driven to Nebraska City in a car operated by her friend Ed Roach. Upon completion of the interview, a reporter called Mr. Roach in Nebraska and he confirmed that he had been in Le Mars on Monday to visit Knox. His story was different from what she had told the reporters, though. Roach said that Knox had been sending him love letters and claiming that she was unmarried, that both of her parents were deceased, and that she was ten years younger than her real age. In one letter, Knox wrote that she "needed lovin' " and requested that Roach come get her. She did add one condition to her offering of love: he had to give her $500 so that she could pay off her mortgage.

No one really knows why Roach went to see Knox that day. He told reporters that he was considering hiring her as a housekeeper, but he may have had more lustful thoughts on his mind. He claimed that Knox did not impress his nine-year-old daughter Geneva, and the two opted to return home without her. This may have been said to save face. Police later discovered bushels of correspondence that Knox had with men all across the country who had been advertising for wives, suggesting that Ed may have really come to Le Mars for the lovin'.

Caught in what was clearly a lie, Knox told the sheriff a totally different story on Friday. "My mother left with Sumner Knox the latter part of May 1938, in a car driven by Clifford Smith, a cousin of Sumner's. They went to Wisconsin—either to Monroe or Janesville." She continued, "I haven't heard from my mother in a long time—I did hear at first, when Sumner took her away... from Janesville, Wisconsin." She claimed that Sumner spiked her mother's tea with sleeping tablets and that he "took [her] mother away from [her] because he said that [she] didn't take the right care of her."

Are you starting to get a sense of déjà vu? First, Knox is found nearly passed out on her mother's bed, then she has two crazy stories to explain it all away. All that's missing from this puzzle is an attempt by Knox to hire an imposter to play the part of her mother.

Shocking as it may sound, it was later learned that she did exactly that. On that first day when reporters arrived at the empty Trow home for their scheduled interview, Knox was really hitching a ride to Sioux City. She lodged with a friend and contacted the local senior home, requesting that one of the women take a taxi to Le Mars to impersonate her mom. Knox was supposedly willing to take anyone, no matter how sick, to stand in as her mother. Her clever plan was squashed when home officials learned of the proposal.

No one believed Knox's latest claim that Sumner had drugged Mrs. Trow, so police asked her to voluntarily stay at a nearby rest home while they continued their investigation. She agreed.

Police were certain that Mrs. Trow had not left home at all. Instead, they believed that she was buried somewhere in the backyard. And how did they come to this conclusion? Let's just say that Knox wasn't very good at keeping her mouth shut. During a conversation with a friend, she remarked, "If they find a body in the garden be sure it is my mother."

On Saturday, November 12, the digging commenced. Behind the house was a garden mound approximately 15 feet (4.6 meters) in length and bordered with bricks. One portion of the mound had sunken in and seemed like the best place to excavate. Less than 2 feet (61 cm) down, a large wooden box was discovered. It was a veneer kitchen cabinet measuring approximately 65 inches (165 cm) in length, 14 inches (35.5 cm) in width, and 18 inches (46 cm) in depth. The shrunken remains of an elderly woman were discovered inside. Knox's brother Len Trow identified the body as that of his missing mom, Lucinda.

Now that the remains of Mrs. Trow had been uncovered, the police wondered whether any additional bodies were buried in that yard, so the digging continued. Dog bones were found in an old well, but no additional remains were found in the garden, human or otherwise.

State toxicologist Wilbur J. Teeters examined the body and reported, "There is no indication of any of the alkaloid or organic poisons." His conclusion was that Lucinda Trow had died of natural causes about six months prior. She was given a proper burial next to the grave of her late husband.

Knox was placed under arrest for illegally burying her late mother and fraudulently cashing in her pension checks. Yet even when confronted with all the mounting evidence against her, Knox still insisted that her husband Sumner and her mom had driven off with his cousin Clifford Smith.

In an effort to leave no stone unturned, investigators attempted to locate this Clifford Smith. Despite so many Smiths residing in the United States, they ultimately narrowed the field down to two different Clifford Smiths who had lived in Le Mars. It was determined that neither had any connection to the case.

Ten days after Mrs. Trow's body was uncovered, authorities learned that Knox had filed papers in Adel, Iowa, on January 21, 1934, charging her husband Sumner with "...cruelty, gambling, non-support and intoxication." The reason no one could find him was that the two had divorced in April of 1934.

On November 30, 1938, Maybelle Trow Knox pleaded guilty
to the charge of conspiracy and was sentenced to a three-year
term in the Women's Reformatory at Rockwell City.

With Knox behind bars and everything she possessed sold off,
there was still one unanswered question in the case: just where
was Sumner Knox?

The answer to this would arrive in the mail on January 11, 1939.
On that day, Plymouth County Sheriff Frank Scholer received
a letter from Sumner himself dated January 8. Sumner was
unaware that anyone had been looking for him. He had been
working for several months in the state of Washington and was
currently in search of additional work. He explained, "So for the
past two months I have been practically out of communication
as to what is going on."

Boy, did he miss a lot...

The Salem Trade School Football Team

1929

Perhaps the worst high school football team to have ever played was located near Salem, Massachusetts. There was a very good reason as to why they performed so poorly, and it had nothing to do with the quality of the team's players.

The 1928 diary of Salem, Massachusetts, resident Stephen Murphy reads like that of any other twenty-one-year-old's. In it, he discussed his concerns over securing a good job, the movies that he saw, and the seemingly endless repairs to his Essex Six automobile. As for his engagement, he briefly wrote on November 7, "Marge got the ring today. Went in with Madeline. She loves it."

At first glance, there seems to be little within Murphy's diary that one would consider out of the ordinary. Yet today, one can find his diary featured prominently in a glass display case on the sixth floor of the Sports Museum in Boston's TD Garden Arena. That's because Murphy's diary is believed to be the only first-hand account in existence of the legendary Salem Trade School football team.

Murphy wrote on September 29, 1928, regarding a meetup at Hudson High School: "We were all equipped. Big crowd there. I did not start the game, but went in at sec. quarter. We won 7 to 0. Hard, clean, fought game." A November 24 entry states, "Catholic High of Revere were the opponents. We won 6 to 0."

Despite these entries, Salem Trade was considered, by far, the worst high school football team in the Boston area. During the nearly six years that the team was active, records show that they won a total of four games. Here is a small sampling of just how bad they were:

October 6, 1928: Weymouth High School beat Salem Trade 13 to 6.

October 30, 1928: Walpole High crushed Salem Trade 27 to 0.

September 21, 1929: Winthrop High defeated Salem Trade 14 to 6.

September 29, 1929: Chelsea High walloped Salem Trade 24 to 0.

What few people realize today is that, back in the 1920s, most schools did not bankroll their sports teams. Instead, they collected funds from sponsors and shared a portion of the gate receipts with the visiting team. The goal was to purchase uniforms and equipment, pay for food and lodging, and cover the cost of transporting a team from one location to another.

The way it worked was quite simple: A coach from one team would contact the representative of another and propose the date, the location, and how much they were willing to pay. If the opposing team agreed to the terms, then the plans would be finalized. Should the offer be too low, the opposing team could either negotiate a better deal or refuse outright.

For example, Murphy wrote on November 7, 1928, "We are planning to get sweaters with the guarantees from the 3 remaining games to be played. At Portsmouth we get $80, Revere, $15.00, Walpole $65.00. Sixteen players, I mean, fifteen, can be equipped for $150. We have not decided on either the color or style, whether roll collar or slip on."

Salem Trade was such a ragtag team that many of its players also took on the duties of running the team. For example, quarterback Harold "King" Burgess was also the team's coach, captain, and manager. Steve Murphy was not only the team's fullback, but he also served as its PR man and helped to arrange games with opposing teams.

He wrote on September 14: "Wrote a piece to Salem News for the Trade School. Two games arranged so far. Practice Sunday afternoon at the Common. I wrote 'Carlin and Rix of last year's freshmen eleven will make a strong bid for a regular berth.' I got quite a kick out of it being in black and white."

The most significant game that Salem Trade ever played was on October 5, 1929, when they shut out Taunton High 6 to 0. One would think that the Salem Trade fans in attendance would have jumped for joy upon witnessing their team's first win of the fall season. But they didn't. There was not one single Salem Trade student in the stands.

Well, maybe no one from the school attended the game. Surely once word got back to campus there would be a celebration of their victory, right? That was not to be, either.

Why? The answer to that question came eleven days later. The shocking news of October 16, 1929, was that while Salem Trade had their own football, baseball, and basketball teams, they didn't actually have a school building. In fact, there weren't any classrooms, administrators, or teachers to teach the classes. In reality, there was no school at all. It was a scam that existed solely to play sports and earn some money.

At no point during the entire time that the team existed had anyone bothered to check and see whether or not Salem Trade was a real school. The fact that the team had never played a home game should have been a tip-off, but no one ever picked up on it.

Murphy's September 10, 1928, diary entry made it clear: "May play football with Salem Trade School this year. I'm going to get Don and Mike on the team. Of course, our school is non-existence [*sic*] but outside schools are unaware of that fact."

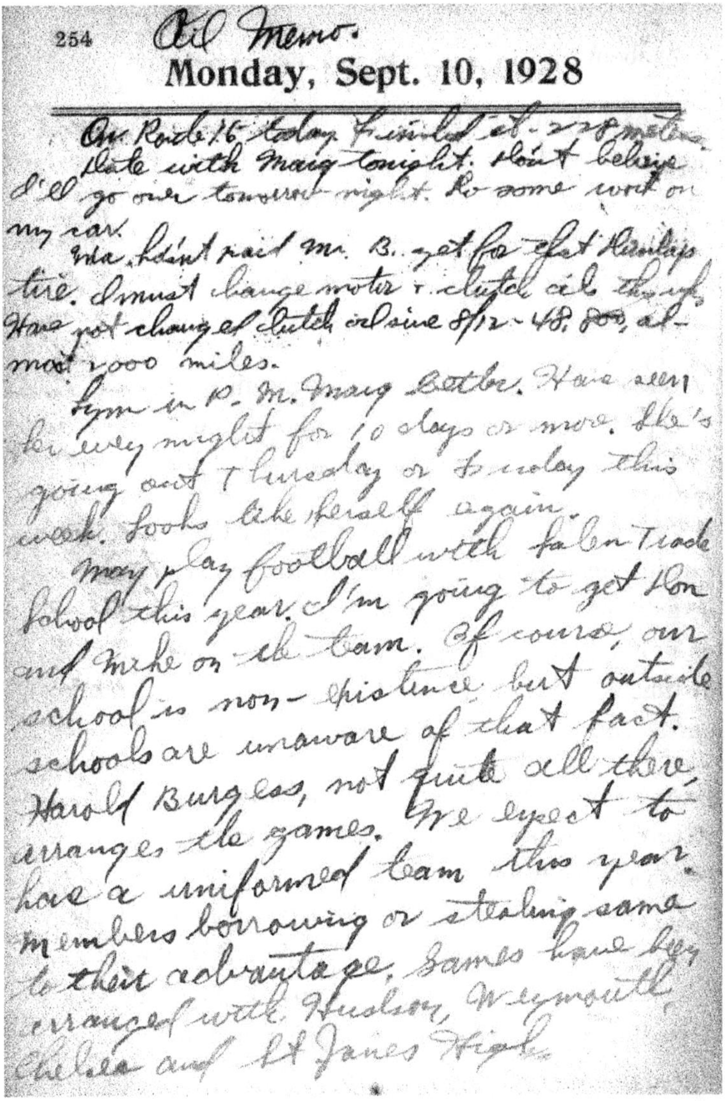

254 Oil Memo.

Monday, Sept. 10, 1928

On Route 16 today finished at 228 miles. Date with Marg tonight. Don't believe I'll go over tomorrow night. Do some work on my car.

Ma didn't [illegible] Mr. B. yet for that Hawley's tire. I must change motor & clutch oil though. Have not changed clutch oil since 8/12 – 48,800, almost 2000 miles.

Gym in P.M. Marg better. Have seen her every night for 10 days or more. She's going out Thursday or Sunday this week. Looks like herself again.

May play football with Salem Trade School this year. I'm going to get Don and Mike on the team. Of course, our school is non-existence but outside schools are unaware of that fact. Harold Burgess, not quite all there, arranges the games. We expect to have a uniformed team this year, members borrowing or stealing same to their advantage. Games have been arranged with Hudson, Weymouth, Chelsea and St James High.

September 10, 1928, diary entry of Stephen Murphy.

His son, John Murphy, told the *Salem News* in 2018, "To me it's a story about Salem, Massachusetts and its uniqueness that only they and the citizens of Salem knew about the team. They all kept it a secret; many people knew it existed, there's no doubt about that. But for a while nobody gave it away."

It was back in 1924 that Harold Burgess noticed a flaw in the gate-receipt-collection system and decided to exploit it. He put together a team of young adults, all of whom had paying jobs. As Burgess received advances for each game played, he paid off the team's expenses and used any remaining funds to line his own pockets.

Burgess had a trick to not getting caught: the players were told to keep the scores realistic, but to avoid winning, as doing so would bring unnecessary attention to the "school."

So who was Harold Burgess? Besides being the superintendent, principal, team manager, coach, captain, and quarterback for the fictitious school, Burgess had completed schooling through the eighth grade and worked as an automobile mechanic. At the time the hoax was revealed, he was twenty-three years old, married, and the proud father of a young girl.

It was that big win on October 5 over Taunton High that triggered the exposure of the Salem Trade secret. After their halfback, Mike Iwanicki, scored the winning touchdown in that game, he demanded that he be paid $10 (about $150 today) per game for his services. Soon, other players on the team requested salaries ranging from $2.50 to $10.00 per game. When Burgess refused to pay up, the players informed the *Boston Globe* of the scam.

"Get this straight," Burgess told the *Boston Globe*, "Before you go saying that I didn't play square with my men, I didn't pay 'em anything to save our opponents from being professionals. If I had paid the Salem Trade gang anything, then everyone, see, everyone, against whom we played would have lost their amateur status. I kept my boys pure so that they wouldn't contaminate the others."

Burgess added, "Sure, some of the fellows were a bit old, but after a year or so we were going to become a college." Apparently, there was nothing in the rule book that could stop a non-existent high school from becoming an equally non-existent college.

Initially there was concern that the team members could face some legal or financial consequences for their part in the scam, but those fears never materialized. John Murphy stated, "Once that story came out, the team members thought that they were going to get in trouble. My father had some pages of his diary ripped out in that same time frame."

Surprisingly, the Salem Trade football team continued. It was announced that they would play a previously scheduled game against Maynard High on November 23, 1929. Maynard's faculty manager and coach Donald Lent stated that, "It would be practically impossible to fill the Salem Trade date with a team of equal drawing power and we are going through with the game."

When game day arrived, only Burgess and one other player remained from the original lineup. Having never practiced together as a team, the Boston Globe reported, "Before the opening whistle Capt. Burgess of Salem Trade team held a reception at a bench on the sidelines in order to acquaint the members of the team with each other." The game ended in a surprising 19-19 tie before "the smallest crowd that has attended a football game here in years."

Harold Burgess

Salem Trade played for another year. On September 20, 1930, Salem Trade shut out Chelsea High 2-0. After that, they lost game after game.

A short, one-sentence statement in the September 21, 1931, *Boston Globe* stated, "Information here in regard to Salem Trade indicates that the team will not operate this season." They would never play another football game.

As for Harold Burgess, he attempted to operate several other fictitious football teams, including high schools in Portsmouth, Rhode Island, and Greenfield, New Hampshire, as well as The Parker School for Boys in Boston. He later moved to Texas.

The *Boston Globe* caught up with Burgess thirty years after they first exposed the fraudulent team to the world, and he offered up the following additional information:

"Nobody ever asked to see the school." He added, "I could have showed them easily enough, if I was forced. I guess I was the only combined principal, coach, and athletic director who carried his buildings, his campus and his faculty around in his pocket."

"It wasn't much of a secret in Salem. They were bound to know that there was no Salem Trade. But mostly they went along. Nobody bothered us, except maybe the cops who used to chase us off the common sometimes when we were practicing."

The only compensation any of the Salem Trade players ever received for their efforts was their team sweaters. On November 30, 1928, Steve Murphy wrote, "Got Sweaters. Look good. Green with a white 'S.' A witch on the arm cost $.50 cents extra. Don [Carlin] got one." His son Paul Carlin was still in possession of that sweater in 2017. Both that sweater and Steve Murphy's diary are now on display at the TD Arena Sports Museum in Boston, Massachusetts.

The Strange Case of the Jitterbug Coal

1944

You've certainly heard about Mexican jumping beans, but have you ever witnessed jumping coal? Such a phenomenon was observed at a schoolhouse. At first, no one could explain why the coal was acting so strangely. Was it alive? Could the school have been haunted?

In January of 1944, the first of about one dozen threatening notes appeared pinned to the door of the one-room Wild Plum Schoolhouse, located approximately 20 miles (32 km) south of Richardton, North Dakota. While the notes' contents were never revealed to the public, they were generally described as "alternatingly threatening and obscene." The only specific detail divulged was that twenty-two-year-old Mrs. Pauline Rebel, the school's only teacher, had been instructed to "leave or be shot."

According to Rebel, in late March, an armed man had been observed outside the school by several students. The man, who stood at approximately 6 feet (183 cm) tall and wore a red bandana to mask his face, kicked the schoolhouse door several times, but ran off before Rebel could get a good look at him.

Things really turned toward the strange on Friday, March 17. A scuttle near the school's stove began to rumble, and pieces of coal started moving around inside the bucket. It seemed as if the coal was alive.

On March 28, while Rebel was administering an arithmetic exam, the bucket of lignite once again began to stir. Suddenly, without warning, chunks of coal "began hopping out of the scuttle like Mexican jumping beans." The lumps flew out with enough force to knock large holes in three of the plaster walls. One piece rebounded and struck student Jack Steiner, and a second hit Rebel. The frightened students scurried under their desks for protection from the flying rocks.

Mrs. Rebel and her students were in a state of terror as nine of the window blinds proceeded to smolder. Smoke was seen seeping from the moldings surrounding the windows. Holes began to burn in the wall map. A built-in bookcase was gutted by fire. Books within the students' desks ignited. A copy of *Webster's Dictionary* smoldered and "exploded." Smoke was also observed emanating from a mail-order catalog.

If this hadn't really happened, one would have assumed they were watching a scene from a horror movie.

Rebel tried her best to calm her students down and then proceeded to call school officials. The first person to arrive on the scene was the father of five of the school's students, rancher George Steiner. He was shocked to find the interior of the school in shambles. He picked up several pieces of the coal and observed that they "were covered with kind of a white dust that looked like talcum powder." One piece violently jumped out of his hand "without making any noise at all."

Students told school officials that they had observed a hooded man racing past one of the school's windows shortly after the pail of coal began its aerial blitz. Suspecting this to be a case of arson, administrators contacted State Fire Marshal Charles Schwartz and asked him to investigate.

A hearing was conducted, during which Rebel and the eight students in attendance that day testified as to what they had observed. Their stories were amazingly consistent. On April 13, Schwartz told the press, "At first we were convinced the whole thing was a hoax and suspected arson, but after we used the lie detector with negative results we are of the opinion that witnesses were telling the truth. To put it mildly, we are puzzled." He added, "We plan to send the pail, the dictionary and a sample of the coal to the Federal Bureau of Investigation in Washington to see if any light can be thrown on the case."

Samples of the coal were also sent to chemists at Dickinson State Teachers College. Preliminary tests found nothing out of the ordinary. It was suggested that the articles that burned within the schoolhouse may have been coated with a chemical residue that could spontaneously combust. Special Assistant Attorney General W. James Austin stated, "Such a liquid could have been sprayed on the curtains, books, maps, moldings [*sic*] and coal and might possibly have produced the reactions reported by the teacher and pupils." He continued, "But we as yet have no way of knowing if that or a similar chemical compound has anything to do with this case."

On April 15, Samuel C. Gordon, curator of minerals at the Academy of Natural Sciences in Philadelphia, offered a possible explanation for the coal's spontaneous ignition. He suspected that the white, talcum-like powder George Steiner observed on the exterior of the coal may have been the mineral melanterite, which forms when surface waters cause pyrite ("fool's gold") to decompose. Entire beds of coal in the Black Hills region of South Dakota had been known to ignite due to a high concentration of melanterite.

With the story making headlines in newspapers nationwide, fear had spread among those living in the area surrounding the school. All fourteen of the enrolled students refused to return, and Mrs. Rebel expressed that she no longer wished to teach there. John Steiner, George's brother, stated, "I won't send my two little ones to school to be scared to death. I don't want things happening that make my children believe in ghosts and witchcraft."

So, what is a school to do without a teacher or any students? Classes were already scheduled to be dismissed on April 28, so the decision was made to simply start the break a couple of weeks early.

Yet, the investigation continued. Fire Marshal Schwartz stated, "We have discarded the idea that it was arson." He added, "If anyone had sought to destroy the schoolhouse by fire he would hardly have employed the use of a chemical such as was apparently used when he could've done the job with kerosene."

Hoofprints discovered beneath the windows of the school were followed to a nearby farmhouse, but were determined to have been created by a stray horse that had roamed the open prairie the previous winter.

Throughout the entire investigation, the students stood up to continued questioning, and their stories remained unchanged. That was, until the evening of Monday, April 17, 1944, when four of the students admitted that they and others had pulled the wool over everyone's eyes.

Here's what really happened:

The masked man seen running from the school was a complete fabrication. The students would pound on their desks and stomp on the floor to give the illusion of someone banging on the school door. The students would then run toward the door and blurt out that they saw a man fleeing. When Rebel would open the door to look for the man, the obscene and threatening notes—which were penned by two girls, aged twelve and fifteen—would be pinned to the schoolhouse door.

As for the jitterbug coal, the students used long rulers to both stir and knock over the scuttle. They also hid pieces of coal in their pockets and desks. When Rebel turned her back toward the students, they would underhandedly throw the pieces of coal at the wall, damaging the plaster in the process.

There was also a simple explanation for all of the fires around the room: matches. The students attempted to set fire to the window shades, the wall map, books, and even the *Webster's Dictionary*.

Investigators concluded that the students meant no harm in what they did. They had a young, inexperienced teacher who, conveniently, was nearsighted. Each time Rebel turned her back or removed her eyeglasses, the students attempted something mischievous. Realizing their teacher was a bit gullible, they made each successive prank more and more outrageous in an effort to convince her that the school was haunted.

In the end, the mysterious happenings at the Wild Plum Schoolhouse were proven not to involve poltergeists, spontaneous combustion, or witchcraft—just a bunch of kids with wild imaginations.

Man Inherits Fortune from Woman He Never Met

1912

The exact date is not recorded, but in the early 1900s, Charles H. Tunley, a Boston dry goods merchant, was walking along Beacon Street when he heard the cries of women in distress. The cries were coming from three sisters—later identified as Miss Mary Brown, Mrs. Jean Hooper, and Mrs. Elizabeth Woodbridge—who were confined in a runaway carriage that was racing down the thoroughfare. Without hesitation, Tunley sprang into action and stopped the carriage. He then assisted the women as they exited the carriage, unharmed, down to the street.

Soon after this event, the three sisters, who were the daughters of wealthy parents, moved to Elford, Essex, England. When the last sister, Mary Brown, passed away in 1905, it was learned that they had left their entire fortune of $3 million ($79 million today) to Charles A. Tunley, son of the man who had saved their lives.

Barrister Henry Hamilton of Elford was named executor of their estate. A search began for the younger Tunley, but years slipped by without him being located. One day, in February of 1912, Hamilton was exiting an elevator of the Standard Oil Company at 26 Broadway in New York City when he overheard a man call out, "Hurry, Tunley, and we'll catch this car." He'd found the man he was looking for.

This incredible story quickly made headlines in newspapers across the country. Yet four months later, Tunley found himself charged for using a forged check to pay his landlord. It was soon determined that his inheritance was nonexistent. It was all one great big lie. He had made up the entire story of the three sisters, their runaway carriage, the barrister's lengthy search for him, and their chance meeting at that elevator.

Two Weeks on Venus

1956

In 1954, Harold Jesse Berney, head of a Washington, DC, television antenna manufacturing operation, said he was chosen by the United States government to be its main contact with Uccelles, a prince visiting our planet from Venus.

In May of 1941, the National Association of Broadcasters estimated that there were only 7,000 television sets operating in the United States, with 5,000 of them in the New York City metropolitan area. As the country entered World War II, the production of televisions, radios, and other consumer broadcasting equipment ceased. Once the war ended, television set sales skyrocketed. There were an estimated 44,000 television sets operating nationwide in 1947, 940,000 in 1949, and a whopping 20 million in 1953. As is the case with all emerging technologies, the years following the introduction of television were exciting and filled with innovations big and small.

Washington, DC, businessman Harold Jesse Berney appeared to be at the forefront of television in the 1950s. His specialty was antenna design. Berney held a 1952 patent for his "Rotatably Adjustable Antenna" invention, plus two additional "Indoor Television Antenna" design patents. He placed the letter A in front of his last name and started the Aberney Corporation, whose sole purpose was the manufacture of television antennas.

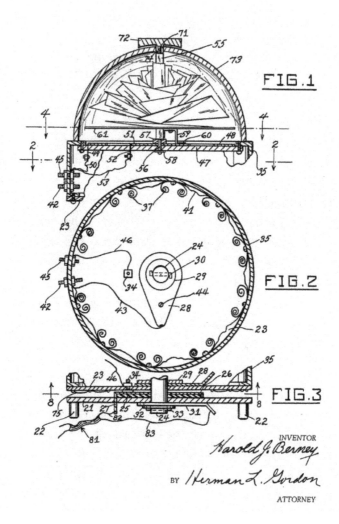

April 22, 1952   H. J. BERNEY   2,594,115

ROTATABLY ADJUSTABLE ANTENNA

Filed May 22, 1950   4 Sheets—Sheet 1

FIG.1

FIG.2

FIG.3

INVENTOR

Harold J. Berney

BY */Herman L. Gordon*

ATTORNEY

Patent 2,594,115 for Harold Jesse Berney's Rotatably Adjustable
Antenna invention.

Berney was in dire need of working capital for his inventions, so in March of 1953, he dissolved the Aberney Corporation and started the Telewand Corporation. His primary backer was a Washington secretary named Pauline E. Goebel, who invested $500 ($4,750 today) into his new venture. In exchange, Goebel was appointed as both secretary and treasurer of the company.

To the casual observer, this was a very good time to be Harold Berney. He had been happily married to his wife Dorothy since the mid-1940s, his daughter Brenda was born in October of 1949, and his son Harold Jr. followed in October of 1951. On the job front, he found an investor who believed in him enough to willingly provide capital for his business. His future seemed very bright.

What few at the time knew was that Harold Jesse Berney had a dark past. First, Dorothy was not his first wife—she was his sixth. At the age of nineteen, he married his first wife Myrtle Alton in Chattanooga, Tennessee, on April 16, 1917. Shortly after Myrtle became pregnant with their first child, two-timing Harry ran off with her fifteen-year-old sister Della. Authorities caught up with the two in Flint, Michigan, where Harold was charged with both taking Della across state lines for immoral purposes and avoiding the draft. He served two years in prison.

After his release, Harold moved around the country and, under various aliases, defrauded people out of significant amounts of money. The specifics of these earlier crimes are beyond the scope of this story, but in nearly every case he got caught, served a relatively short stint in prison, and, upon release, ripped someone else off.

Looking back, it should come as no surprise that Pauline Goebel would lose a fortune investing in Berney's television antenna business. What was most surprising was *how* it happened. Harold Jesse Berney was about to pull off one of the most bizarre cons ever attempted.

***

In the summer of 1953, Berney told Goebel that he was going on vacation with his wife and two children to Rehoboth Beach in Delaware. What he didn't mention was that it was less of a family trip and, at least to a con man, more of a business trip. While there, he met Pleasant McCarty and his wife and told them about a patent he had just received. He described the invention as phenomenal, one that was capable of drawing endless energy from the atmosphere, and said that the Westinghouse Electric Corporation was in talks to purchase it from him.

Assuring the couple that they could quickly triple their money, Berney convinced them to part with $10,000 of their hard-earned cash. They then took out a mortgage on their business so they could invest an additional $10,000. The following January, Berney got them to part with yet another $2,000, to "help meet business expenses." Like those who keep company with any great magician, the couple never saw Berney and their $22,000 again. In today's dollars, the McCartys were out more than $200,000.

And here's where the story gets bizarre. Having rapidly burned through the McCartys' investment, Berney needed a new sucker to milk dry. He set his sights on someone he knew well—Pauline Goebel.

He wove a fanciful tale that took advantage of the public's incredible lack of scientific information about outer space. Given the fact that man had yet to fly into space, humanity's collective imagination was filled with incredible stories about UFOs, Martians, and other aliens.

While we now know that Berney was down in Delaware that previous January defrauding the McCartys, he told Goebel that he had been on a top-secret mission. The mission was so hush-hush that only the White House, the top executives at Westinghouse, and a few top government officials were in the know. He revealed this information to Goebel in the strictest confidence, and warned that she couldn't repeat what she knew to anyone.

He told her that instead of going to Delaware, the government had flown Berney and Westinghouse officials to a military base in Houston, Texas. He went on to explain how the group first walked through a series of buildings before emerging onto an airstrip, and said what they saw there was beyond belief. It was a humongous, bell-shaped flying saucer that Berney estimated was about 30 to 40 feet (9 to 12 meters) tall, and 100 feet (30.5 meters) in diameter.

Berney told Goebel, "because of the high regard which officials of the federal government have for me, I was asked to enter first." He added, "Inside the saucer I heard a voice. The voice said that I had been chosen as the representative of Earth for the planet Venus. After a brief conversation, the voice became a visible blue glow—and the blue glow suddenly changed into the form of a human being."

This interplanetary traveler introduced himself as Prince Uccelles. He informed Berney that his home planet wished to establish a relationship with the United States and to share their technological advances. Their only requirement was that it all be kept a secret.

Once the meeting concluded, Berney and the head honchos of Westinghouse flew back to Pittsburgh, where Berney checked into a hotel. That evening, Prince Uccelles—who claimed to be six hundred years old—magically reappeared and told Berney about a "modulator" that his people invented to extract energy from the Venusian atmosphere.

This fantastical new machine could do so much more than what it was capable of when he ripped off the McCartys. Berney said that it could "softly lift and lower millions of tons in a fraction of a second. It can propel planes and space ships at the speed of light—or hold them motionless in the sky. It produces a power potential far greater than anything your atomic energy can contrive."

Goebel was sold on the idea and jumped at the chance to invest more of her money. In exchange for every $100 invested, she received a stock certificate representing one share in the Telewand Corporation. Once he suckered her in, Berney left on another one of his so-called business trips.

On April 5, 1955, Goebel answered the telephone in her Washington, DC, residence. The call was from a stranger in Texas claiming to be Prince Uccelles himself, and he told Pauline that Berney was on Venus seriously ill. He called again the next day and told her that Berney had died. Goebel should have questioned why an alien allegedly capable of transforming into a blue light and teleporting himself just about anywhere would use a lowly telephone, but she didn't. She bought the story hook, line, and sinker, and quickly jumped into action. Recalling that only a select few had knowledge of the US government's contact with Venus, she urgently tried to call President Eisenhower to let him know of Berney's passing.

This should come as no surprise, but she was unable to get in touch with him.

About one week later, Goebel discovered a handwritten letter penned by Uccelles on her desk: Berney, who was supposedly dead, was now in need of money. "I will be able to give him $500 which will tide his small bills, but he will need about $3,000 for the others."

Five months later a second letter appeared—Berney required additional funds. Goebel sent $4,500 to the Texas address indicated.

On October 4, a third letter arrived in the mail informing her that Berney had "passed through a complete process of regeneration." Having fully recovered, he was currently en route from Venus back to Texas.

***

Harold J. Berney was alive and well when he returned to Washington that fall. After having made a brief stopover on the moon, he returned to Earth via a two-mile-long (3.2 km) spaceship. He told outrageous stories of his experiences on Venus and extolled the advancements of Venusian technology. Buildings soared taller than the Washington Monument. So plentiful was gold that it was used in the manufacture of ordinary bathroom fixtures. Crime was non-existent and punishable by extradition to another planet.

Berney wanted to share his extraordinary Venusian experiences with the world and, with Goebel's secretarial assistance, he began work on a manuscript titled *Two Weeks on Venus*. The book, however, was never completed.

Once again, during the summer of 1956, Berney was called away to Pittsburgh on business. Upon his return, he reported that, though the technical problems with the modulator had been resolved, the changes weren't being implemented fast enough. Though he lacked the capital to do so, he promised ten Westinghouse executives a bonus of $1,000 each if they could get them done by an agreed-upon deadline.

Hmm? Where could he quickly come up with that kind of cash? Any ideas?

Goebel wrote him a check for the $10,000. This would be the last of her business dealings with Berney.

Later that fall, Berney's wife Dorothy received a package in the mail that had been postmarked as having been sent on November 13, 1956, from Eagle Pass, Texas. Inside she found Harold's wallet, about $300 in cash, all of his credentials, a camera, his watch, and a tie pin & cuff links set that bore the initials HB. More significantly, there was a note hand-scribed on parchment paper telling Mrs. Berney that her husband had died and his body was lying in state on Venus. It was signed by the one and only Uccelles. Unlike Goebel, Mrs. Berney didn't believe any of it and was convinced that, instead of dying, her husband had deserted her and their children.

In February of 1957, the FBI became involved in the case. They were certain that there had been no Venusian modulator, no dealings with Westinghouse, no trips to Venus, and no Prince Uccelles. Harold J. Berney was also nowhere to be found.

The FBI did have a few clues to help track down Berney. First, between swindles Berney had legitimately worked as a sign painter. They also determined that after he checked out of a hotel in Pittsburgh, Pennsylvania, he purchased $600 worth of sign-painting supplies. Finally, Berney was known to head south and spend winters in warmer climates. This all added up, and the FBI focused their attention on sign painters in southern states.

On March 21, 1957, an FBI agent in Mobile, Alabama, learned that a 1955 Oldsmobile had been registered under the name Hal Berney. Agents drove over to Berney's home in nearby Pritchard and found a newly established sign-painting company located there.

No one was there at the time, but a neighbor identified Berney as the home's occupant. The neighbor suggested that the still married Berney might be over at his fiancé's house. As investigators drove to her residence, they spotted a man that fit Berney's description behind the wheel of an Oldsmobile and signaled for him to pull the car over. Berney was arrested but denied the charges. He was quoted as saying, "Trip to Venus? Why that's ridiculous!"

Smooth-talking Harold Berney couldn't wiggle his way out of this one, as the evidence against him was overwhelming. He pleaded guilty to the charges and was sentenced to a term of twenty months to five years in Florida's Raiford Prison.

The exact date of Berney's release is unclear from available government documents, but it is known that his last employer was the Patrick Sign Company in Rockville, Maryland. He succumbed to congestive heart failure on December 19, 1967, at sixty-nine years old.

Pauline Elizabeth Goebel was ninety-three years of age when she passed away on February 25, 1997, in Silver Spring, Maryland.

When everything was totaled up, Berney had defrauded Goebel out of an estimated $38,000 and the Delaware couple out of an additional $22,000. Adjusted for inflation, his cosmic con raked in nearly $570,000. Not bad for two weeks on Venus...

1957 image of Harold Jesse Berney.

The Crayola Caper

1973

The Concord Hotel in Kiamesha Lake, New York, was once the largest resort in the Catskill Mountains. Few people remember today, but it was once central to one of the most bizarre extortion schemes ever.

When I was seven years old, my parents made the decision to move from Brooklyn to the tiny town of Thompsonville, New York. I've always joked that Thompsonville was so small that, if you blinked while driving through, you'd miss it entirely.

Yet, our home was not as far removed from the rest of the world as one would believe. We lived in the heart of the Borscht Belt, the portion of the Catskill Mountains nicknamed for its high concentration of Jewish hotels. By the time I was a teenager, nearly all of these resorts had either declined significantly or shut their doors entirely. There were many grand hotels, but none as large as the Concord Hotel in Kiamesha Lake, which was a short drive from my parents' home.

On June 30, 1973, a photocopy of a letter was mailed from a Manhattan post office to Robert Parker, the general manager of the Concord Hotel. The four-page, typewritten, single-spaced document was highly unusual, not solely for its content, but for the fact that it was signed in orange crayon with the pseudonym "Crayola."

The letter threatened to taint the coffee and drinking water of one hundred hotel guests with the hallucinogenic drug LSD. Since the Concord's main dining room could seat up to 3,000 people, Crayola wrote that this was enough to trigger "a runaway chain reaction of exponential proportions with the dosed victims in a state of neuron-splattering terror."

Yet, there was a way that the Concord could prevent this from happening. The letter requested that, on July 6, 1973, a female hotel employee take $320,000 ($1.83 million today) in old $100 bills, evenly divided between two TWA airline travel bags, to a telephone booth located on the corner of 45th Street and Fifth Avenue in New York City. Further instructions would be provided there.

Postcard image of the Concord Hotel.

Parker was cautioned by Crayola not to contact the FBI under any circumstances. "A word of warning—so much as *entertain* the notion of trying to put us out of business, and highly motivated associates of ours will descend upon you with orders to annihilate." The letter continued, "If you want to think that all this is just one great big sick hoax...think again." Further, "If you are tempted to gamble that we're just bluffing...think of what happens to other people's brain tissue if you're wrong."

The hotel went against Crayola's advice and immediately contacted the FBI. Unaware that the feds had been contacted, two follow-up telegrams were sent to the hotel. A July 3rd message authorized a 10 percent reduction from the original $320,000 if the hotel did not contact the "constabulary," and a July 5th telegram warned that once the "toothpaste" was out, it could not be put back into the "tube."

At 3:15 p.m. on July 3, FBI Special Agent Margot P. Dennedy, posing as a Concord Hotel employee, stood in front of the designated phone booth with the two TWA bags hanging from her shoulders. The phone rang and the caller asked Dennedy for the code word. She replied with "Crayola," and the game began.

Dennedy was directed from one phone booth to the next, unaware that her actions were being watched by Crayola, who was perched above her on the second floor of the nearby Pan Am (now the MetLife) Building. Upon entering Grand Central Terminal, Dennedy was directed to a phone beneath an advertisement poster, coincidentally for Concord watches.

Directly behind Dennedy was a restroom with a sign that read, "Ladies Room Closed. Use Upper Level." She was instructed to walk toward that door and shove the two bags of cash through a small opening where a piece of glass had been broken out. Dennedy did exactly that. What she couldn't see on the other side of the door was that the two bags had fallen onto a small rug with a piece of rope attached to it.

As soon as the drop was made, three FBI agents descended on the bathroom, only to find that the door was locked. What they couldn't have known at the time was that after the bags were pushed through the door, Crayola's female accomplice pulled on the rope to slide the bags to the back of the restroom. In the process of doing so, one of the bags fell off the carpet. When the FBI began pounding on the door, Crayola's associate panicked and opted to leave the second bag behind. She escaped via a rear staircase that connected to the upper-level ladies' room. A few minutes later, the FBI agents gained entrance to the bathroom and found it to be completely abandoned.

***

Only time would tell if the suspect had made a clean getaway. After leaving Grand Central, the accomplice met up with two more co-conspirators. The three then took a taxicab to the East New York Savings Bank located at East 64th Street and Third Avenue. Upon entering the bank, they proceeded to safety deposit box 338, which had been rented three days prior under the aliases of "Calvin Morrow" and "Robert Diamond." But when they opened the TWA bag, they discovered that it contained fake money, and that the FBI had concealed a transmitter in the strap of the bag. The three immediately discarded the transmitter and later boarded the Staten Island Ferry, from which they dumped the bag of bogus bills into the river.

Crayola was now in a state of panic. Not only did they fear the FBI had tracked them from the taxi directly to the bank, but Crayola also worried that his fingerprints were on the safety deposit box application and could be linked to his US Navy records. In an effort to cover up their misdeeds, Crayola concocted a plan in which they would pretend that the whole extortion scheme was politically motivated and not intended to harm anyone.

Two weeks later, Crayola sent the FBI an angry letter in which he claimed that the entire Concord-LSD threat was a hoax. It was a test set up to see how the FBI would handle the situation, and they failed miserably. "The Bureau blundered disastrously [*sic*] and irretrievably by substituting fake money for real." He continued, saying that this was "irrefutable proof of the Bureau's knowing, deliberate and wanton engandering [*sic*] of hundreds of unsuspecting guests at the Concord." He warned that if the FBI didn't immediately release psychedelic drug guru Timothy Leary—who had been serving two ten-year sentences for marijuana possession—Crayola would reveal to the press how utterly incompetent their agents had been.

When Leary wasn't released, Crayola wanted to prove to the FBI that his threat to publicly release the story was serious. Crayola started small and placed an advertisement in the *Village Voice* that mocked the feds. The ad certainly got their attention, but nothing changed.

In late September, the Washington, DC, office of syndicated newspaper columnist Jack Anderson received a call from someone named "Spendlove," who had an improbable story to tell, and an appointment to meet was scheduled. On Friday, September 28, a man dressed in a flowered shirt and bell-bottom pants walked in and sat down with Anderson's associate, Joseph Spear. Spendlove proceeded to tell his story about how the FBI had mishandled the Concord extortion plot. Spear was skeptical and asked for proof, but Spendlove lacked it at the time. As the meeting ended, Spendlove identified himself as Crayola.

On October 3, 1973, Spear received a call from Crayola stating that he could provide a copy of the extortion letter as evidence. Crayola then contacted his male accomplice in New York and requested that he obtain the original letter from the safety deposit box and make a copy.

Two days later, on Friday, October 5, as he was exiting the bank with the original extortion letter in hand, the FBI swooped in and arrested a nineteen-year-old college student named Robert E. Greenman of Flushing, Queens. Later that day, forty-year-old John Calvin Van Orsdell (sometimes reported as Vanorsdell), a.k.a. Crayola, was apprehended in Philadelphia. Their female accomplice was later identified as twenty-year-old Inese Gerke.

According to court documents, the FBI had been on Van Orsdell's tail for more than a month. A confidential source provided Van Orsdell's name and that he had visited a bank on East 64th Street. Investigators obtained lists of those who accessed their safety deposit boxes on the day of the crime and found one that most likely belonged to Van Orsdell. They concluded this by examining "Calvin Morrow's" completed application. Morrow and Van Orsdell shared a birthdate: August 23rd. Both had parents named Mary and Edward. Lastly, Van Orsdell's middle name was Calvin.

Van Orsdell was indicted on February 22, 1974. When the trial commenced in Manhattan Federal Court on November 6, Van Orsdell admitted that he had written the extortion letter to the Concord, but stuck to his story that it was all a hoax designed to both expose the FBI for its shabby investigative procedures and secure the release of Timothy Leary. Noting that he was a "middle-of-the-road radical," he told the jury, "I must admit I am drawn to things like that. It was all words: the idea of committing extortion from money is abhorrent to me." After exposing the FBI for its ineptness, his ultimate goal was to secure book and film rights for his story.

The prosecution argued that Van Orsdell's radical FBI defense was designed to cover up his disastrous attempt to extort money from the Concord Hotel. They pointed out that Van Orsdell was a struggling author who, excluding his 1971 novel *Ragland*, had all his works consistently rejected. At the time of his arrest, Van Orsdell was heavily indebted for back rent and additional unpaid bills. It was noted that the $30,000 ($171,000 today) invested in a production company he formed were squandered on rent, a Caribbean cruise, and a trip to London.

Most damaging of all were the testimonies of his unindicted co-conspirators, Gerke and Greenman. Both recalled that Van Orsdell had concocted the politically motivated scheme the night following the failed Concord payoff attempt.

On November 15, 1974, the jury returned a verdict of guilty on all charges. Van Orsdell faced a maximum of twenty-five years in jail and up to $15,000 in fines, but Judge Whitman Knapp went easy on him. On January 10, 1975, Van Orsdell was sentenced to two years in prison, to be followed by five years of probation.

An appeal was immediately filed, and the defense's main argument was that Van Orsdell had been illegally monitored by a recording device. When the evidence was presented in court, it was learned that only Special Agent Dennedy's voice could be heard on the telephone recordings. In addition, the transmitting device that the FBI placed in the strap of the TWA bag had failed the moment it hit the bathroom floor in Grand Central Terminal. On September 8, 1975, the United States Court of Appeals, Second Circuit, affirmed the decision of the lower court.

PART 5

HEROES & SURVIVORS

The Rescue of Charles Nalle

1860

The amazing story of the only person in the United States to have been rescued from slavery four times.

My wife and I live a short distance from Troy, New York, and it is among our favorite small cities to visit. There are many reasons for this, but much of our enjoyment is derived from Troy's spectacular architecture and rich history. One can hardly walk anywhere in the city without finding something of historical importance.

The corner of State and 1st Street is one such place. There you'll find the Mutual Bank Building, an ornate brick structure that once housed the Bank of Troy in the mid-1800s. Today, it is home to a law firm and, if you didn't look carefully, you'd have no clue that one of Troy's most significant historical events occurred right at that spot. The only hint is a small plaque affixed to a wall at the far end of the building that reads:

HERE WAS BEGUN APRIL 27, 1860 THE RESCUE OF CHARLES NALLE AN ESCAPED SLAVE WHO HAD BEEN ARRESTED UNDER THE FUGITIVE SLAVE ACT

The story of Charles Nalle began in 1821, when Peter Hansbrough, a plantation owner in Culpeper County, Virginia, purchased a slave at auction. Her name was Lucy, and the sale included her four children, the youngest of whom was Charles. While it cannot be said with certainty, it has long been thought that Nalle was one of a large number of children that Hansbrough fathered throughout his lifetime.

On January 31, 1831, the elder Hansbrough transferred ownership of Nalle to his son Blucher, and it was said that the two bore a strong resemblance to one other. Being owned by his half-brother brought Nalle privileges that few slaves ever had. While he did occasionally work on the plantation, most of the time he worked in the house as a servant, cared for the horses, and, as a coachman, accompanied Blucher to places far and wide. When Nalle reached adulthood, Blucher permitted him to marry Catherine "Kitty" Simms, a slave on a farm approximately three miles (4.8 km) away.

In 1847, Blucher Hansbrough decided to sell off some of his slaves. Several days later, a fire desroyed one of his barns and consumed most of the harvested wheat crop. Hansbrough suspected that it was done in retaliation for the pending sale, and that one of his slaves was responsible.

Nalle, two of his brothers, and three additional slaves were ordered to enter the farm's mill as the doors were shut behind them. The six men were beaten, handcuffed, and placed aboard a boxcar destined for the slave market in Richmond, Virginia.

On the day of the auction, bidders were scarce. Two of Hansbrough's field hands sold immediately. When Nalle was placed on the auction block, the highest bid placed was $650 (about $18,000 today)—below the price that Blucher desired. The same occurred with the three remaining men. As a result, they all remained unsold, and Hansbrough returned the next day to take them back to his plantation.

Then, in May of 1855, something shocking happened. Kitty's owner, Colonel John Triplett Thom, died, and his will called for all twenty-nine of his slaves to be emancipated. Kitty and the couple's four daughters were now free.

For most slaves, this would have been a dream. And yet for Charles and Kitty, it proved to be a nightmare. Under Virginia law, all freed slaves had to leave the state within one year or they risked being re-enslaved. For Kitty, this meant potentially being sold down the river and never seeing her husband again. On the other hand, if she moved to a free state, there was an equally high chance of them being kept apart forever by the distance.

The couple realized that there was only one solution, and it was a risky one. On May 21, 1856, the couple and their children moved to Washington, DC, which still had slavery but permitted freed slaves to live there as long as they carried their free papers. Anyone that lost those papers for even a moment would be re-enslaved.

With Kitty now emancipated, Nalle's friends attempted to purchase his freedom. One offered $700 and included a free black man in exchange as security. This would allow Charles time to earn the funds needed to pay off the balance owed. Unfortunately, Hansbrough declined and set his asking price at $1,200. This was considered an astronomical amount and the deal fell through.

In early October of 1858, Nalle informed Hansbrough that Kitty was very sick and could die. As this was a time of great turmoil in the slave states, he cautiously gave Nalle and another slave named Jim Banks a one-week pass to visit Kitty in the nation's capital. The two never got there.

On October 15, 1858, Nalle and Banks were able to give their chaperones the slip and began their escape to freedom. Nalle ended his dangerous journey in Albany, New York, about 8 miles (12.9 km) south of Troy. Infuriated by their escape, Hansbrough sold Nalle's two brothers and another man off to a plantation in Alabama.

It was later learned that Nalle had arranged his escape with a man named Minot S. Crosby, a twenty-six-year-old missionary from Massachusetts. Crosby had been teaching at a school in Culpeper but was, in reality, working there as part of the Underground Railroad. Around the time of Nalle's escape, Minot's actions came under suspicion and he was forced to flee.

After he arrived in Albany, the Underground Railroad found Nalle a job in nearby Sand Lake, New York. His coachman skills came in handy as he gained employment trucking lumber from the sawmills. For lodging, he was able to stay with a family that had also recently relocated to Sand Lake: the family of Minot S. Crosby.

In his spare time, Nalle was determined to learn how to read and write—skills that were denied to slaves under Virginia law. This venture would prove to be a big mistake.

Somehow, the contents of a letter Nalle had sent to his family came to the attention of a twenty-five-year-old lawyer named Horatio F. Averill, who had previously been forced to leave a New York City law firm for suspected embezzlement. Averill decided that he should contact Hansbrough and inform him of the location of his runaway slave. In exchange for Hansbrough retaining him as council, Averill assured the return of Nalle. (Side note: today, the town of Averill Park, New York, is named after him.)

In early April of 1860, Nalle relocated to Troy and secured employment as a coachman for Uri Gilbert, one of the city's wealthiest industrialists. Charley, as many in the city now called him, boarded with William Henry, a black man who operated a grocery store a short distance from the Gilbert mansion.

At 11:00 a.m. on April 27, 1860, Nalle was sent by Mrs. Gilbert to procure some bread at a nearby bakery. While sitting on his wagon outside the bakery with the reins in his hands, he was grabbed by two men who came at him from behind. They were Deputy United States Marshal John L. Holmes and Jack Wale, a slave catcher hired by Hansbrough to bring Nalle home.

They shackled Nalle and took him to the local office of the US Commissioner, located on the second floor of the Mutual Bank Building. Representing Blucher Hansbrough were the scoundrel Averill and another lawyer named William Beach. As for the commissioner who would decide Nalle's fate, he just happened to be William Beach's son, Miles Beach. Nalle didn't stand a chance.

In reality, it made no difference that the Beaches were related to each other. Under the Fugitive Slave Act of 1850, it also didn't matter whether or not Nalle was in a free state. Federal law treated escaped slaves as the property of their owners, no matter who they were or where they resided.

While the hearing was held to determine the fugitive slave's fate, one of Gilbert's sons became concerned when Charley didn't return from his bread run. After finding Nalle's abandoned wagon, Gilbert went to William Henry's grocery in search of him. Gilbert and Henry soon learned from witnesses that he was being held at the commissioner's office.

Henry and some friends quickly went to the office of Martin Townsend, a lawyer for the Underground Railroad. He raced over to the commissioner's office and, upon gaining entry, learned that an adverse decision had already been made. Townsend knew there was little that could be done, but he needed to stall for time. He told Commissioner Beach that he would be back shortly with a writ of habeas corpus.

What no one had anticipated was the reaction from the citizens of Troy. A large crowd began to form outside the commissioner's office. Henry addressed the growing crowd and informed them that Charley would probably be sent back to Virginia and whipped to death solely because he desired being a free man.

No one was sure of exactly what was going on up in the commissioner's office until a woman snuck upstairs and acted as a lookout. As long as the crowd could see her, they were assured that Nalle was still in the building. That woman would later be identified as Harriet Tubman, who had coincidentally made a brief stop in Troy while on her way to an abolitionist meeting in Boston.

Around 3:30 p.m., a heavily handcuffed Nalle was able to nudge a window open in an attempt to jump down to the street. Cries of "Let him down!" "Come, old boy!" "Catch him!" and "That's it!" could be heard from the crowd below. He had one leg out the window and was preparing to leap just as someone pulled him back inside.

Townsend arrived back at the commissioner's office at 4:00 p.m. with the writ of habeas corpus. It required that Nalle appear before Supreme Court Judge George Gould a couple of blocks away. Today, Russell Sage College occupies that site.

By this time, the crowd had grown to an estimated two thousand people, so leaving the premises was not easy. With city policemen there to assist, Marshall Holmes and Deputy

Sheriff Nathaniel Upham firmly held on to Nalle as they led him down the stairs to the street below. As he emerged from the building in shackles, Tubman screamed, "Here they come!"

The mob rushed in. Marshall Holmes and the other officers were struck several times as the crowd tried to drag Nalle away. There was so much pushing and pulling that it seemed as if he would be torn to pieces. Soon, Deputy Sheriff Upham was forced to let go of the prisoner.

As Marshall Holmes struggled to escort Nalle to the next block, there was one person who would not let go. That person, again, was Harriet Tubman. She told the crowd, "Drag us out! Drag him to the river! Drown him! But don't let them have him."

The struggle continued. At one point, an officer drew his revolver, pointed the barrel at a rescuer's head, and threatened to pull the trigger. A member of the mob then forced the officer's arm up into the air as another held a knife against his throat.

The crowd succeeded in pulling Nalle away. He was rushed down the street to the eastern bank of the Hudson River, placed in a skiff, and rowed to the opposite shore. There, a sympathizer jumped in the water and pulled him out of the boat. Nalle then headed up the embankment alone.

His freedom did not last long. A message was telegraphed ahead that Nalle had escaped and that he'd be setting foot on the opposite shore shortly. Plus, the sight of a bloodied, handcuffed man walking along the main street of West Troy (today Watervliet) was certain to grab attention. Ten minutes after breaking free of officials in Troy, Nalle was once again arrested. This time he was hauled to the second-floor office of

Justice Daniel C. Stewart. (Today, a McDonald's restaurant sits on that site.)

As Harriet Tubman and others watched the arrest from the opposite side of the river, they could feel the result of their valiant efforts slipping away. Just at that moment, a steamer docked at Troy and the mob ran toward it. Those who were unable to board the steamer commandeered nearly every other available boat. Within minutes, a small armada of several hundred people made its way across the Hudson River. As soon as they touched the West Troy shoreline, they made their way to the brick building where Nalle was being held.

The crowd gathered outside as Tubman and others made their way upstairs to the locked door of the judge's office. One after another, they hurled stones at the door. A constable fired shots, and bullets passed through one man's hat and coat, but caused no harm. The rocks continued to fly. More bullets were fired. One wounded a cigar maker in the thigh. Another took off a small slice of a farmer's cheek.

Once the mob had made its way into the office, they seized Nalle, quickly led him down the stairs, and carried him along the road to the US Army's Watervliet Arsenal, which is still in operation today. Nalle was then loaded onto a wagon as the mob fought off those in pursuit. He was driven some six miles (9.7 km) away before a stop was made to have his shackles cut. It wouldn't be until his arrival in Schenectady at 11:00 that evening that the cuffs would be completely removed. Nalle ultimately found refuge in Amsterdam, NY, some 30 miles (48 km) northwest of Troy.

Yet, he still was not a free man and was at great risk of being recaptured. The citizens of Troy and West Troy needed to make one final rescue. This time they took a less violent approach:

they raised $650 in an attempt to buy Nalle's freedom. Luckily, Hansbrough was in no position to negotiate and agreed to draw up emancipation papers.

Charles Nalle returned to Troy on Friday, May 25, 1860, as a free man. Gilbert gladly offered him his old job back. Nalle would be reunited with his family a few weeks later and, for the first time ever, they all lived together under the same roof.

Shortly after the Civil War ended, Nalle, Kitty, and their eight children moved to Washington, DC. There he worked as a postal carrier, and Kitty as a seamstress. He lived there until his death on July 13, 1875, and the story of his dramatic rescue faded into history for fifty-seven years.

On August 9, 1932. Nalle's son, seventy-seven-year-old John C. Nalle, was passing through Troy on his way to vacation in Saratoga Springs, NY. He was asked to be the guest of honor at a ceremony being held at the corner of State and 1st Street. It was there, standing beneath the plaque that bore the name of Charles Nalle, that he learned of the valiant rescue that had taken place seventy-two years prior to save his father from the chains of slavery. Not once had Charles ever told his children anything about the events that had secured his freedom.

HERE WAS BEGUN
APRIL 27, 1860
THE RESCUE
OF

CHARLES NALLE

AN
ESCAPED SLAVE WHO HAD BEEN
ARRESTED UNDER THE
FUGITIVE SLAVE ACT

PLAQUE RESTORED BY
NORSTAR BANK
RENSSELAER COUNTY HISTORICAL SOCIETY
TROY-COHOES YWCA
VERSATILE CLUB
FEBRUARY 1987

Plaque commemorating the rescue of Charles Nalle located at the corner of State and 1st Street in Troy, NY.

Upon returning home to Washington, DC, John began work on a book about his father's life. It was never to be completed. During the evening of July 29, 1934, while staying at the former summer home of abolitionist Frederick Douglas in Highland Beach, Maryland, John Nalle passed away.

Perhaps the best way to end this story is with the words of Charles Nalle himself. He penned a note of thanks to the people of Troy, the conclusion of which was published in the June 7, 1860, edition of the *Troy Daily Times*:

> "And as to my late master I owed him nothing, but he in truth owed me all, for I was the robbed man—robbed all my life, and instead of him receiving remuneration, that remuneration should have in justice been given to me; but, however, I will leave that to the justice of another day."

"And I say again to those sympathizing gentlemen, from the bottom of my heart I thank you, and trust that, as through the exceeding kindness of Mr. Gilbert, I am able so early to bring my family to the city, that good conduct, earnest and meritorious endeavors may ever characterize me and mine, and prove that this act of public generosity, of Christian magnanimity and kindness exercised on our behalf, may not go unrewarded."

Incredibly powerful words...

It Doesn't Always Pay to Be a Hero

1957

Advertising executive Lowe Runkle was driving his car on Saturday, April 13, 1957, in Oklahoma City when he spotted a young boy trying to break free from a bulldog that had clamped its teeth into his leg. Runkle quickly brought his car to a stop, jumped out and grabbed the boy. He managed to shake the dog loose, but while doing so, tripped over the dog and fell to the ground.

Runkle immediately stood back up and moved the boy, seven-year-old Bruce Allen Pitts, into his car. Before he was able to shut the door, the dog leapt into the car. Runkle grabbed hold of the dog and pulled him out. While he did this, the boy, remembering that he should never get into a stranger's car, exited out the other side.

After hearing the commotion, the boy's mother called the police believing that her son was being kidnapped. From her point of view, Runkle was the kidnapper and the dog was her son's savior.

Unaware that the police had been contacted, Runkle continued his attempt to keep the dog away from the boy and, while doing so, the dog bit *him* on the leg.

It was only when Runkle was being treated at the hospital for his own minor wounds that people determined he was the real hero.

Perhaps it is true that no good deed goes unpunished.

Beached Steel

1868

*Nothing on earth is permanent. As sure as there are forces
that push mountains upward, there are opposing forces
that will eventually bring them all back down. And no
matter how hard humans may try, nature always wins
in the end.*

Located just slightly south of the intersection of Avenida Las
Dunas and Calle Pacífico Norte in Arica, Chile, lies an unusual
rusting mass surrounded by a post-and-chain fence. This
structure consists of a cylindrically-shaped central portion with
a large opening in its top, supported by two large rectangular
structures that radiate outward on the sand floor below.

At first glance, one would guess that these were the remains
of a military tank. Upon further investigation, you may
conclude that this is what remains of some sort of an industrial
plant. Yet both are incorrect. What's harder to believe is that
on June 4, 1984, this rusted mass was declared a National
Historic Monument.

To understand why this pile of decaying steel is of such great
importance, one needs to turn the clock back to August 13,
1868. It was a beautiful day, not a cloud in the sky. Everything
seemed peaceful as the twenty-five thousand residents of Arica
(still within Peruvian territory at the time) went about their
daily routines.

Then, at approximately 5:05 p.m., the ground started to shake.
There was a loud rumbling noise and within minutes, the
entire city of Arica was lying in ruins. Without any warning,

an earthquake had leveled the city. Today, scientists estimate
its magnitude to have been between 8.5 and 9.0 on the
Richter scale, ranking it as the sixth most powerful recorded
earthquake since the year 1500. As the earthquake's energy
radiated outward from the epicenter, it traveled up and down
the Pacific coast of South America, causing extensive damage
to coastal villages and towns throughout southern Peru and
northern Chile.

Panic immediately set in among survivors. Those who
witnessed the horror from ships anchored in the harbor began
to send men ashore to help in the rescue effort.

Then, shortly after the earthquake concluded, the water in
the harbor began to recede. Rear Admiral L. G. Billings,
who was aboard the *USS Wateree* in the harbor when the
earthquake struck, described to *National Geographic* in 1919
what occurred next: "But our troubles then commenced. We
were startled by a terrible noise on shore, as of a tremendous
roar of musketry, lasting several minutes. Again the trembling
earth waved to and fro, and this time the sea receded until the
shipping was left stranded while as far to seaward as our vision
could reach we saw the rocky bottom of the sea, never before
exposed to human gaze, with struggling fish and monsters of
the deep left high and dry."

In 1868, these destructive, seismic sea waves were nearly
unheard of. Today, people would know this sudden drawback
of the shoreline to be a clear signal of an impending tsunami.

As the sea came roaring back in, the water began to pile up
on the shoreline. Estimates of the wave's height have varied
greatly, ranging from 40 to 70 feet (12.2 to 21.3 meters) tall.
Anything in Arica that was left standing after the initial shock
was now swept away by the giant wall of water. The tsunami

raced across the Pacific at a speed in excess of 500 mph (805 km/h), and even produced considerable damage in such distant places as Hawaii and New Zealand.

Rear Admiral Thomas Turner of the South Pacific Squadron, in his September 3, 1868, report to the US Navy, described what remained of Arica: "The upper part of the city, which from its elevation escaped the encroachment of the sea, has not a single house or wall left standing—it is in one confused mass of ruins, more or less in every part prostate; whilst the lower part, which comprised chiefly the better and more substantial order of edifices, including a large custom-house of stone mason work, is literally as perfectly swept away, even the foundations, as though they had never existed, and present the appearance of a waste that had been ravaged by the waters of a mighty river, carrying everything before it in its irresistible volume."

In addition to the destruction on the shore, boats and ships had sat on the newly exposed ocean floor were suddenly picked up and tossed around like pieces of cork bobbing on the water. While most of the larger ships in the harbor were able to ride out that wave, smaller boats were not as lucky.

And things were about to get far worse. When darkness set in, a lookout aboard the *Wateree* reported another large wave approaching. It was a second tsunami, even greater in amplitude than the first.

Once again, we turn to Admiral Billings and his telling of the story in *National Geographic*: "Looking seaward, we saw, first, a thin line of phosphorescent light, which loomed higher and higher until it seemed to touch the sky; its crest, crowned with the death light of phosphorescent glow, showing the sullen masses of water below."

As this second wave rolled in, the ships that had survived the previous tsunami were no longer so lucky.

Most notable of these was the *USS Fredonia*, which the US Pacific Squadron had permanently stationed in Callao, Peru, as a supply ship in 1862. To avoid the ravages of yellow fever, the *Fredonia* was towed by the *Wateree* to Arica six weeks prior to the earthquake. Unfortunately, the *Fredonia* did not survive the tsunami—it capsized, taking $1.8 million in stores (roughly $34 million today) and the lives of twenty-seven people down with it. There were five survivors: three officers who were onshore at the time and two men rescued from the wreckage the following morning.

The Peruvian corvette *America* was severely damaged by the wall of water and eventually came to rest on the beach. Sadly, the thirty-three people aboard the ship did not survive. The *Chañarcillo*, a barque out of Liverpool, was reportedly destroyed as well, and much of its crew lost.

Yet, there was one ship left mostly intact that reported no loss of life: the *USS Wateree*.

It was the *Wateree*'s unique design that saved it. Built near the end of the Civil War, the ship was never used for its intended purpose—to navigate the shallow, meandering rivers of the southern United States. For that reason, the *Wateree* had a flat bottom and was propelled by a sidewheel. Since turning a ship as large as the *Wateree* around in a narrow river was difficult, the front and rear of the ship were identical, and included a rudder at both ends. The *Wateree*'s flat bottom allowed it to come to rest in an upright position as the tsunami drained the water out of the harbor. It was this feature that all the other ships anchored at Arica lacked, causing each of them to roll onto their sides as they were set down on the dry seabed.

At the onset of the quake, ship commander James H. Gillis gave the orders to batten down the hatches and set the anchor. When the first tsunami hit, the second anchor was dropped, but the water's incredible force tossed the *Wateree* violently before temporarily setting it down on the beach. With the next wave crest, the ship was once again afloat, allowing the *Wateree*'s crew to rescue those from other boats that drifted by when water levels fell.

When the second tsunami hit, the *Wateree* was rapidly pulled seaward and swung around wildly. It was nearly tossed on its side but soon righted itself, and dragged its anchors before coming to rest. Commander Gillis later told the Navy, "I have had the height to which the solid sea wave rose measured, and find that it is 42 feet and 5 inches, and the wash is from 10 to 15 feet higher." At sunrise the next morning, it was finally clear that the *Wateree* would never sail again. It sat nearly 450 yards (411.5 meters) inland and three miles (4.8 kilometers) north of Arica.

The *USS Wateree* (left) stranded on the beach at Arica, Chile. The Peruvian corvette *America* is visible in the distance.

Since the *Wateree* was mostly intact, it was set up as an emergency hospital to help survivors of the earthquake. The *USS Powhatan* picked up the crew a few days later and returned them to the United States.

On November 21, 1868, the *Wateree* was sold at auction for $2,775 (approximately $53,000 when adjusted for inflation). It was used as a hotel, a nightclub, once more as a hospital, and finally as a storage warehouse.

On May 9, 1877, another major earthquake struck Arica. The resulting tsunami briefly refloated the *Wateree*, but by the time it was set down farther southwest, the ship had been destroyed. Now much closer to the ocean, the effects of time, looters, and those who used the *Wateree* for target practice left nothing but its rotting boilers behind. In an effort to protect what little remained, the *Wateree* was moved to the island of Alacrán, but the constant attack of waves and salt accelerated its decay.

In 1998, the Consejo Provincial de Monumentos Nacionales (Provincial Council of National Monuments) decided to move the *Wateree* farther inland, away from the water, where it resides today. The remains of the *USS Wateree* can be seen on Google Maps at -18.441806, -70.303194. Those coordinates place you at the exact location of that rusting mass mentioned at the beginning of this story.

Mystery solved.

Falling Girl
Saved by a Spike

1911

Seventeen-year-old Ida Singer had been working on the ninth floor of the Triangle Shirtwaist Factory for six weeks when a fire broke out on March 25, 1911, and killed one hundred and forty-six garment workers. It remains the deadliest industrial fire in New York City's history.

"When I first heard the alarm," she said, "I was paralyzed with fear. I was too weak to run. I half crawled to a back window and I remember I was crying as I raised a window opening on the narrow fire escape. Flames were roaring out of the windows below, but I knew I had to go down the narrow fire escape and climbed down. I turned around and saw many girls rushing toward the window I had gone through. I was glad they were coming and stopped crying."

"I felt I had to get down ahead of them. The iron steps of the ladder was hot and getting hotter as I went down. I had taken probably three steps downward when the first of the girls rolled out of the window above me crashing down on me, and I lost my balance and felt myself falling. I remember I was almost glad of it before I lost my senses."

"When I woke up I was in the funniest position. I had to stop and study it out. My hands were down by my feet and I was doubled up." She continued, "I tried to move and couldn't. After a long time I heard a voice and a window was open. Two men got hold of me and took me inside the building. My coat, skirt and hat remained on a big spike in the wall."

"But I shall never forget what I saw below me when I was hanging on that spike. I saw men and women piled up on top of one another. Some were quite still and others were frantically waving their arms and shouting. I saw a girl wiping a man's face with her handkerchief. After a while they all quieted down."

The Last Man Standing

1885

*Nearly everyone wishes for a long, healthy, happy life.
But a long life will most likely make you outlive everyone
you know, which begs the question: is living a long
life worth it?*

Following the Confederate attack on Fort Sumter on April 12,
1861, President Abraham Lincoln called for a 75,000-man
militia. Eighty-nine men in and around Stillwater, Minnesota,
volunteered to form the Stillwater Guards, who marched off
to war as Company B of the 1st Minnesota Volunteer Infantry.
These brave men fought in three major battles: the First Battle
of Bull Run, Antietam, and Gettysburg. Only forty-three of
them survived.

In 1885, the surviving members of Company B held a reunion
at the Sawyer House Hotel in Stillwater. They agreed to meet
back each year on July 21, to commemorate the day they went
into the First Battle of Bull Run.

While they weren't the first or last group to come up with the
idea, a member of the group suggested that they start a Last
Man's Club. At this club, a chair would be set out for each of
the thirty-four surviving members of Company B. Once a man
passed on, that soldier's chair would be draped in black crêpe.
When the last man remained, he was to stand up and make a
final toast to all of his fallen comrades.

In 1887, Louis Hospes, father of member Adolphus C. Hospes,
donated a "large and commodious bottle of wine" to be
consumed by the last man standing. Between the club's annual

meetings, the bottle was stored at Stillwater's First National Bank, of which the elder Hospes was president. Member Henry C. Van Vorhes arranged for the construction of a lined box in which the bottle would be stored. Inserted into the box were the words to the "The Last Survivor," a poem penned by Stillwater resident H. E. Haydon.

As time passed, the number of survivors slowly dwindled. The first man to pass away was William Morgan in 1888. Three members, including Van Vorhes, were next in 1889. The number continued to shrink, with one or two members passing on each year. Yet there were gaps. For example, not a single man died from 1896 through 1901. Fast forward to 1920, and a total of five members passed on in that single year, leaving only five of the original thirty-four men still alive.

While the press annually printed small blurbs about the club's meetings, their interest in it greatly increased after the meeting on July 21, 1923. The president of the organization, Adam Marty, had died the previous winter, and left the club with four surviving members. Eighty-four-year-old Peter Hall, the oldest of the group, was selected as their new president. With Hall now in charge, one of the three other members needed to fill his former secretarial post. Emil Graf was ill and not in attendance, so the job would fall to either Charles Lockwood of Chamberlain, South Dakota, or John Goff, who resided at the Minnesota Soldiers Home. Lockwood nominated Goff for the position. Goff, in turn, nominated Lockwood. It was up to the president to cast the deciding vote. Hall flipped a coin and Mr. Goff was elected secretary.

Members of the Last Man's Club in 1917. Left to right: Adam Marty, Peter Hall, John Goff, and Charles Lockwood.

At that same meeting, Hall stated, "Our Constitution provides that the last man shall attend the annual banquet as usual, and drink a toast to his dead comrades. With this rite he will close the books on the Last Man's Club. But it has occurred to me, as perhaps it has to you, that that last banquet would be a sad occasion, and I want to make a suggestion which we can decide at our next meeting. That is that the last two men shall drink the toast and break up the club." They also discussed whether the bottle of wine should be resealed and donated to the Stillwater post of the American Legion once the club's final toast had been made.

A big change came in 1924. The Sawyer Hotel, the site of their annual meetings, was closed and scheduled for demolition. The reunion was thus moved to First National Bank Building. As was the case the previous year, Emil Graf was too ill to make the trip. At a large table with thirty empty chairs shrouded in black crêpe, the three in attendance agreed that the last two survivors should share in making the final toast.

The 1925 meeting was more of the same, though it was reported that their annual toast was made with everyone seated because one member was unable to stand without assistance.

Emil Graf passed away on March 5, 1926. Another chair was draped at the club's meeting later that year.

As each surviving member aged, it became increasingly difficult for them to get together. In a show of respect, an estimated five hundred people witnessed the 1927 ceremony of the Last Man's Club. The three final men mutually agreed that it was time to formally disband. As they looked out over the thirty-one pall-draped chairs, the bottle of Burgundy wine—held in trust since the very beginning—was finally uncorked. Peter Hall, the only man to sample from the bottle, announced that the wine had turned to vinegar. A final toast was made, and the bottle was sealed back up and returned to the bank vault for safekeeping.

The fact that alcohol had been consumed during Prohibition did not go unnoticed. On July 22, H. T. Laughbaum, superintendent of the Oklahoma Anti-Saloon League, called the Last Man's Club "a bad example to the youth of the country. Men who have fought for their country ought to respect its Constitution."

But that final formal meeting did not bring an end to the Last Man's Club. The three simply opted for a more private affair. In both 1928 and 1929, they met at the St. Paul home of Mrs. William Griff, Goff's daughter.

Sadly, the three would never meet as a group again. Eighty-six-year-old John Goff passed away on August 28, 1929, at the Veterans Hospital in Fort Snelling, Minnesota. Both Lockwood and Hall were in attendance at his funeral. Not long after that, on April 18, 1930, Peter Hall died at his Atwater, Minnesota, home.

Charles Lockwood was now the last man standing. At Peter Hall's funeral, Lockwood stated, "We had seen so many others fall that we had begun to think that we possessed charmed lives." He added, "Each year since there has been a reunion, more chairs draped in black have been added as we sat down to live over the old memories. But the last years I think we have all wondered as we sat smiling that probably next year our chair would hold only crêpe. But next July 21, always our meeting day, I will go to the old Sawyer house in Stillwater, where we first met, and carry out my pledge."

And then the day came. On July 21, 1930, Charles Lockwood made his way to the Lowell Inn, which stood on the site of the old Sawyer House. Inside, he stood at the head of a long table surrounded by thirty-three empty chairs. As the roll call commenced, the first thirty-three names read were met with silence. When the last name on the list was announced, Lockwood stood up and stated, "Present." He then lifted his glass of vintage wine and proceeded to read the last portion of H. E. Haydon's "The Last Survivor":

"I hear no answer to my call,
    the glasses stand filled to the brim;
From out of the sky, upon the wall,
    no shadow falls of face or limb;
Turn out the lights, the feast is o'er;
    no answer in my calling comes;
I stand beside a fast-closed door:
    my pulses beat like muffled drums.

The camp-fire smoulders, ashes fall,
   the clouds are black athwart the sky;
No taps of drum, no bugle call—
   my comrades all, good-bye, good-bye!"

Charles Lockwood then took a sip of the wine and made the final entries into the club's record book. Forty-five years after their first reunion, the Last Man's Club had passed into history.

Seventy years after he first fought on the battlefields there, eighty-eight-year-old Charles Lockwood returned to the nation's capital to participate in the Memorial Day services at Arlington National Cemetery. As he stepped off the train in Washington, DC, on May 7, 1931, he was greeted by reporters.

When asked about the wine supposedly tasting like vinegar, he reached into his pocket and pulled out a small bottle of the liquid and said, "That's it! Taste it for yourself. Vinegar, humph! It's Burgundy—and good enough for Burgundy. But I've always thought it was foolish to have wine. It should have been good Irish whisky!"

With regards to the club itself, he stated, "It makes a fellow think—watching them drop out that way, one at a time." He continued, "But getting together that way every year kept us mighty close. We didn't forget much. That's why I'm going over the whole ground again."

As he approached the Lincoln Memorial, Lockwood noted, "I remember the first time I saw Abe Lincoln. It was on Arlington Heights—a grand review. He sat on a fine black horse, with his plug hat set back, like this—," at which point Lockwood pushed back his gray cap. He continued, "And that plug of hair of his was hanging down like this. I thought he was about the homeliest man I ever saw in my life. Once I called on him and shook hands with him—that was after Bull Run. He was always kind to all the soldiers and glad to see them."

Lockwood returned to Stillwater in 1931 and 1932 to make his annual toast to his fallen comrades, but in 1934 announced that he was unable to attend.

Captain Charles M. Lockwood, the last man of the Last Man's Club, passed away at the Minnesota Soldiers' Home Hospital in Minneapolis on October 4, 1935. He was ninety-three years old.

Can't Take It Anymore

1936

Every year since 1928, the Jumping Frog Jubilee has been held in Angels Camp, California, to commemorate Mark Twain's 1865 story, "The Celebrated Jumping Frog of Calaveras County." The winner of the contest is the frog that jumps the farthest from the starting point to the final landing position of its third jump.

The 1936 grand champion was a frog named Can't Take It. On May 17, Can't Take It made a three-hop total distance of 12 feet, 3 inches (3.73 m).

While caged in the Pasadena yard of George W. Conn, Can't Take It apparently decided that he couldn't take it anymore, and on June 11, the frog made a giant leap for freedom.

Luckily, three weeks later on June 21, Can't Take It was recaptured ten blocks from where he had escaped. It was the frog's big booming voice that led rescuers to him.

PART 6

NEWSWORTHY: PAST & PRESENT

The Average Man

1927

How would you describe the average man? Clearly, there is far more to him than physical characteristics like height and weight. In 1927, a search was held to find the man who best typified the average male.

"He must be an American citizen of average size, average education and with an average viewpoint. He must own an average home on an average street, drive an average automobile and be the head of a family of four. He must neither be in the employer class nor yet in the employee class. He must be neither a leader nor a laggard in public affairs; neither prominent nor obscure; neither the most popular man in town nor the most unpopular."

I must admit, this sounds quite a bit like a description of me. It's not. But it is *how* William S. Dutton, writer for *American Magazine* in 1927, described his national search criteria for the average man. The methodology used to identify the average man was quite straightforward:

1. Divide the United States population by the number of states (48 in 1927).

2. Using that calculated value, see which state's population was most numerically similar.

3. Divide that state's population by the total number of cities and towns in said state.

4. Identify which city or town has a population similar to that value.

Using the estimated populations at the time of this writing, the average man in the United States would now be located in SeaTac, Washington, a city that did not exist in 1927.

Dutton concluded that Fort Madison, Iowa, was the location where the average man could be found. He claimed that Fort Madison not only had the average population of an American town, but it also had an average geographical location and an average climate.

After Fort Madison was selected, next came choosing the average man. (It was clearly a sign of the times the average woman wasn't sought out at the same time.) This task was given to the residents of Fort Madison. Using the Dutton's list of specifications, they chose Roy L. Gray as their average man. Upon being chosen, Gray commented, "I know I am an average man, but why pick me out of a hundred million?"

"Average Man" Roy L. Gray in 1932.

Gray, the proprietor of a men's clothing store, was average in nearly every way. He was of average height and build, had an average education, lived in what was described to be an average home on an average street, drove an average dark blue car, and was the head of a family of four, which was the average family size used by the Census Bureau at the time.

As for his interests, Gray stated, "Most of all, I am interested in my home. And next comes my business because my home depends upon it." Beyond that, Gray was only moderately interested in things that went on in the world around him. "I read the newspaper like anyone else. I look at the front page, and I always get to the 'funnies' sooner or later."

His taste in music ranged from the modern jazz of his day to light classical compositions. "When I first got the radio, I sat up nights trying to get distant places. But I got over that long ago.

Now I tune in on the stations that I know have good programs and stick to them. I don't 'fish around.' I listen in on important speeches, and if the speech isn't good I simply tune it out."

Roy was a registered Republican who always voted along party lines in national elections, but considered himself to be independent on local issues. He was a member of a church, but did not attend services on a regular basis. Gray belonged to the local Chamber of Commerce, as well as the Elks, Odd Fellows, and Rotary clubs.

Within a week of being named the average man, Gray's story made front-page headlines in thousands of newspapers. "I thought newspapers printed only pictures of important people or great criminals. But, no matter. I'm average enough to enjoy the thought of seeing what my face will look like when it comes out in print."

In one article syndicated by the United Press, Gray was asked to answer a series of nineteen questions on a wide variety of topics. Here is a sampling of them:

Question: "Who is the greatest living American?" Answer: "Lindbergh."

Question: "Do you personally believe in the theory of evolution?" Answer: "No."

Question: "Who is your choice for president, and why?"
Answer: "Hughes is best qualified from every viewpoint."
(He is referring to Charles Evans Hughes, who was later
appointed the 11th Chief Justice of the United States
Supreme Court.)

Question: "Do you approve of smoking by women?"
Answer: "No."

Question: "Do you think present styles in women's dress
tend to cause loose morals?" Answer: "No."

On October 21, 1927, Gray traveled by train to Chicago,
courtesy of the *Chicago Herald and Examiner*, to experience
what a big city was like. Ever the family man, his first task was
to purchase a postcard with a photograph of his hotel on it to
send back home. Before mailing, he marked the location of
his room on the 30th floor and wrote, "This is where I slept.
Having a good time but wish you all were here."

As you would expect, his first full day in Chicago began with
an average breakfast: eggs, toast, coffee, and a cigarette. He
received a shave and then went off to meet the mayor, William
Hale Thompson. From there, he was taken to what was then
known as the world's busiest corner: that of State and Madison
Streets. He commented, "Whew! You know in Fort Madison
we don't have any stop and go lights or traffic policemen. Don't
need 'em except on Saturday night when the stores stay open
and everybody comes to town."

Later in the day, Gray took a visit to the Board of Trade to see
"the pit" where stocks and commodities were traded. "Gee, you
can't hear yourself think." He continued, "I'd rather have my
little one-man store back in Iowa and be sure of a bank balance

at the end of the year than risk any money on this game. I think you've got more suckers in Chicago than we have out our way."

Next up was steak-and-potato dinner back at the hotel, followed by a show to finish off the evening. At this point, Gray was exhausted. "Well, I sure had a fine time," he told the press. "My feet hurt me a bit but I'll soak them in hot water. I see there is a Bible in my room. I'll read myself to sleep."

With all this wining-and-dining, one had to wonder if the average man was still, you know, average. Only time would tell.

While Gray was in Chicago, the press didn't ignore his wife, Etna, back home in Fort Madison. As you would expect, Mrs. Gray was average in size, moderately attractive, and wore clothes that were fairly up-to-date, but not overly tight-fitting. Like most housewives of her time, she did her own housework and cared for their children, eight-year-old Dick and four-year-old Sue. Like most parents, she wished for both of her children to not be average. "We want them to go further than we have."

"I know what Roy is doing in a general way, but I attend to the house, and he to his business, and that way we get along." She continued, "It keeps me pretty busy just looking after all the details of running a home. That, you know is a real job, a job for any real woman."

As for her husband's newfound fame, she stated, "Just the same I don't like to think of Roy as being the 'average man,' because I think he is more considerate and more thoughtful than the majority of husbands. We're not rich and we're not poor, but we are content to go ahead just as we always have. Contentment is happiness, you know."

On October 26, Gray returned from Chicago to his average home on that average street where he was greeted by his average wife and average children.

One year later, it was obvious that the fame of being the country's average man had not changed Roy Gray in the least. "Change?" Gray told the press, "What I can't figure out is why so many folks got the notion that I was going to change." When asked if the publicity had been a help or hindrance, he replied, "Well, I am sure that it helped my business. And a lot of people speak to me now where two years ago I could walk to work without meeting more than two or three persons with whom I was personally acquainted."

While some considered him a fool for not cashing in on his fame, he had no regrets. "Yes, I probably could have made a lot of money," Gray noted. "I could have made money by saying that a hair tonic I had never used has kept me from going bald, and for testifying that one bottle of patent medicine had cured me of an ailment I never had. And I could have made a pretty snug sum by going onto the stage—a promoter in Chicago actually started to draw up a contract for one thousand dollars a week. But there're other things in the world bigger than money."

When asked what these things were, he replied, "Plenty of them. One of them is the respect of the folks you live with and meet every day on the street. I'd rather have them say that my word is good than make a million."

Two years after being named the average man, Gray's attitude was still upbeat. "No, I'm not tired of being the average man, neither am I tired of hearing about it. There is never a day that I do not hear at least one reference to it." One thing that did change in his life was that he had purchased a new automobile—an average car, of course.

"Being the average man has had its drawbacks," Gray pointed out. "There were hundreds of people to shake hands with me. There were hundreds of letters from all over the world asking for everything from autographs to money to old clothes. The letters still come, but not so many of them."

When the third anniversary of being coined the average man arrived in 1930, the press was once again there to interview Gray. "Some writers have suggested that I should resent the fact that I was named 'average.' I do not. I am proud of the distinction and would not take a good deal for the experience it has brought me."

Yet by late July of that same year, it was clear that he was growing tired of the spotlight. He opted to refuse all picture taking and interviews with reporters.

As the Great Depression settled in, Gray was forced to cut prices at his store. It was noted that in 1930, his suits were lowered from about $33 to $26 each ($500 to $400 today). He also had to advertise and work more. "I am the proprietor, general manager, and head salesman, and I do the sweeping out."

While he voted for Herbert Hoover in the 1928 election, he did not believe that Hoover could get reelected in 1932. Gray was correct that Hoover would lose, but was wrong in stating, "I think the Democratic nominee will be some man who has not yet been mentioned. I don't think it will be Franklin D. Roosevelt, Alfalfa Bill Murray or anybody like that, but some 'dark horse' who will sweep the Chicago convention. He should be a type of man like Theodore Roosevelt; that's what this country needs today, a real leader." FDR won.

As time went on, Roy Gray was mentioned less and less in the newspapers. And as is the case with all men, average or not, no one lives forever. He passed away on October 2, 1963, at seventy-nine years of age—well above the average life expectancy of a male born in 1884.

One-a-Day Triplets

1950

Lester and Mabel Hardie were already the proud parents of seven children that ranged in age from two to fifteen years when they learned that Mabel was pregnant with twins. They all lived in a 40-foot (12.2 m), four-room houseboat anchored in the Ouachita River, approximately 4 miles (6.4 km) from the nearest hospital in Jonesville, Louisiana.

Early in the morning on Tuesday, March 7, 1950, Mrs. Hardie felt ill. Mr. Hardie took her downstream to the hospital. It was there, at 8:00 a.m., that Dr. N. G. Nasif delivered a 5-pound (2.27 kg) baby boy. The couple named him Jodie Lee. The next day, Mrs. Hardie again gave birth—this time to a 6-pound (2.72 kg) girl, Julie Fae. Then on Thursday, to everyone's surprise, a 7-pound (3.18 kg) girl, Judie Mae, was born at 12:15 p.m. All were healthy.

It was the first set of triplets Dr. Nasif had ever delivered. He stated, "I examined her and knew twins were coming, but the third child surprised me, and the father was really upset." He added, "After the second one, I thought I was through... But by golly, I wasn't. I came back the third day and had to do the whole thing all over again."

Mrs. Hardie described the birth of her triplets as "about the longest and most miserable hours [she] ever spent."

A total of fifty-two hours passed between the birth of the first and last child. In addition, they were the first known triplets in medical history to have all been born on different days.

Ferryboat O'Brien

1952

The strange, true story of Michael Patrick O'Brien. He belonged to no country, and it seemed as though he'd be stuck sailing the same back-and-forth trip every single day for the rest of his life.

Have you ever wondered what it would be like if every single day you woke up was a repeat of the last? That was the premise of one of my favorite comedies of all time: 1993's *Groundhog Day*, starring Bill Murray. Every morning, weatherman Phil Connors awoke at 6:00 a.m. to the sound of Sonny & Cher singing their 1965 hit "I Got You Babe," only to quickly realize he was reliving Groundhog Day for the umpteenth time.

On September 18, 1952, a man named Michael Patrick O'Brien found himself in a similar situation. Every morning at 5:00 a.m., O'Brien would wake aboard the ferryboat *Lee Hong*, wash and shave in the men's room of the ship's ballroom, get dressed, and just sit around all day with no place to go and absolutely nothing to do. At 11:00 p.m. each evening, he would lie down on a leather sofa in the lounge, fall asleep, and begin the routine again the next day, and the next, and the next.

Michael Patrick O'Brien aboard the ferryboat *Lee Hong*.

It's not that the ship wasn't going anywhere. The *Lee Hong* made one round trip daily between Hong Kong and the former Portuguese colony of Macau, a 40-mile (64 km), four-hour trip each way. Three months later, he found himself still aboard the *Lee Hong* and stuck in a nautical yo-yo. He had logged nearly 6,000 miles (9,656 km), including nineteen days that he was stuck aboard the ship while it was drydocked for its annual inspection.

The problem was that O'Brien truly was a man without a country. With the last name O'Brien, the Red Cross said he was Irish. O'Brien stated that he was actually born in the United States, but the US claimed he was from Hungary. Hungary also denied that he was one of their citizens. As a result, he lacked a passport and visa, so neither Macau nor Hong Kong allowed him to set foot on their soil. This sentenced O'Brien to a perpetual ferry-go-round between their two ports.

O'Brien's dilemma was first picked up by various news services in early October of 1952, and was closely followed as he logged additional days at sea. On December 25, his older brother Michael (his real name) came forward after seeing various pictures of him in newspapers, and stated that Michael Patrick O'Brien was really Stephen Stanley Ragan. He wasn't certain, but he believed that Steve was born in Poland and came to the United States at around seven years of age. One week later, another older brother, Los Angeles school custodian Joseph Ragan, positively identified O'Brien as Steve and declared that he was born in Tacoma, Washington, in 1905. Neither brother was correct.

Determining exactly who Stephen Ragan was and how he became Michael Patrick O'Brien has proven to be extremely difficult. As he assumed multiple aliases throughout his lifetime, the few documents available on him today are widely inconsistent. Much of what is known comes from what Ragan himself told the press, and his life story varied with each retelling.

In an August 21, 1953, interview with the United Press, he stated, "I'm an American all right but the State Department says I came here from Hungary when I was two years old and that I'm named Istvan Ragan. Whatever anyone says, I'm an American." Assuming this statement is correct, immigration records indicate that three-year-old István Ragán arrived from Hungary aboard the *SS Slavonia* on May 24, 1907, along with his thirty-eight-year-old mother Anna and seven-year-old brother Josef. The document indicates that they were headed to Tacoma to meet up with Steve's father, Andrew. The 1910 US census confirms that the couple and their seven children, all from "Aust. Slovenian," were together in Tacoma.

A large family doesn't always make for a happy one, and
the Ragan household proved to be an example of that. Dad,
accompanied by one of his sons, went back to Hungary "to fight
the Hussars." Another son was killed in a train wreck. And
then there was Steve, the black sheep of the family. "I never
did get along well at home. For one thing, the old lady spoke
Hungarian. And I never did learn the lingo, so we couldn't talk
to each other except through my sisters. Hell, they shipped me
off to a detention home before I was seven and then sent me to
truant school for a couple of years."

Upon leaving the reform school at age thirteen, he went to work
in a Rainier, Oregon, window and door factory, after which he
found employment as a waiter aboard a steamer that cruised
between Seattle and Alaska. Eight months later, he turned to
playing pool and fleecing others, but "the sheriff ran [him]
out of town."

In 1919, he joined the Army as a cook but deserted after one
year. His next stop was the Navy. He joined using the alias
Robert Stephens, but a friend warned him that the Army was
hot on his trail, so he arranged for a discharge. He opted to hide
in plain sight: he headed to West Point and rejoined the Army
as Robert Stephens. Four months later, he was caught and
General Douglas MacArthur, superintendent of the military
academy at that time, recommended a prison term of ten years
for desertion. Years later, Ragan stated, "I've never forgiven
MacArthur for that." A one-year sentence was ultimately
handed down, which he fully served.

Jobs were hard to come by after his release, and Ragan hooked
up with a gang that was caught in the act of stealing bales of
silk. For that crime, he was given a two-and-a-half- to five-year

term at Sing Sing. He was released after eighteen months and decided to move back to the Pacific Coast.

On September 17, 1926, Ragan married Violet M. Delfel in Vancouver, Washington. The marriage certificate indicates that he was twenty-two and she was eighteen. "The way she was stacked I thought she was about eighteen or nineteen. Turned out she was only fourteen." He was once again in a hot mess. Ragan was arrested and charged with violating the Mann Act, which forbade the transportation of women over state lines "for immoral purposes." Since Violet wished to stay married, however, the charges were later dropped.

September 17, 1926 marriage certificate between Violet M. Delfel and Stephen S. Ragan.

He returned to a life of crime and committed a few more holdups before getting caught again. After his partner in crime turned state's evidence, Ragan was sentenced to twenty years in the slammer. While he served his time, his wife Violet passed away on April 21, 1930.

Ragan claimed that after serving six years of his sentence, the warden at the state penitentiary in Salem, Oregon, informed him that they were pardoning foreigners, provided that they leave the country. On October 20, 1931, Stephen Ragan was deported from the United States.

With a criminal record and no passport, there were few places Ragan could go. Hungary didn't want him, so he set his sights on Shanghai, boarded a ship, and worked his way across the Pacific. Since he lacked the necessary paperwork to gain admittance into Shanghai, he threw a rope over the side of the ship, lowered himself onto a small Chinese boat, and snuck ashore.

In 1932, Ragan purchased a set of identification papers off a man for $50 (approximately $930 today). From that day forward, Stephen Stanley Ragan came to be known as Michael Patrick O'Brien.

In the 1930s, O'Brien found employment in gambling halls, as a bartender, and as a manager of nightclubs. During World War II, he was imprisoned in a Japanese concentration camp in China. Once the war ended, he worked quite a bit on merchant ships. O'Brien may have spent a significant time at sea, but he had good reason to return to Shanghai: he met and married a significantly younger Russian woman named Helen, who had given birth to their child—a son named Patrick—in July of 1947.

By the spring of 1949, it was incredibly difficult for non-Communists to find work in China, so one of O'Brien's friends arranged for him to work aboard his boat, the *Laura Pattison*, which he was to meet in Macau. The Portuguese granted him transit papers, but when O'Brien got to Macau, the boat was gone. Press reports differ on why he never boarded that ship—he either missed it, or it was no longer seaworthy and had to be junked. But without a ship, the Portuguese claimed that O'Brien had entered their colony under false pretenses and they gave him five days to get out.

With nowhere to go, O'Brien jumped aboard the *Lee Hong* ferry and headed for Hong Kong, where British authorities also denied him entry. This brings us full circle to O'Brien literally going around in nautical circles.

***

On March 21, 1953, six months after he first set foot on the *Lee Hong*, O'Brien refused to pay his food bill and the captain called the Macau police aboard to force payment. O'Brien, whose former *Laura Pattison* employer had been providing him a small sum to cover his expenses, refused to pay because he felt that the food wasn't "fit to eat."

He was thrown in the brig and stayed there until the morning of July 30, 1953. It was then that Hong Kong police boarded the ship and informed O'Brien that his wife Helen had moved to Brazil several months prior and filed an application with authorities there asking for him to be allowed to do the same. Brazil, with the encouragement of several refugee agencies, agreed to allow his entry. After ten months and twelve days, O'Brien finally said goodbye to the *Lee Hong*. The following day he flew to Rome, hopped a train to Genoa, and then set sail for South America aboard the French liner *Bretagne*.

Upon his arrival in Rio de Janeiro, O'Brien was told that Brazil had reversed its decision and that he would be required to stay aboard the *Bretagne*. He believed that this was "because some low-down, crummy magazine writer had put in that [he] was a white-slaver and dope peddler." He denied the charges and stated, "I don't wear any blooming halo. I know that. But most of the stuff that's been printed about me is lies."

When the ship docked in its next two ports—Montevideo, Uruguay, and Buenos Aires, Argentina (its final destination)—both countries refused to grant O'Brien admittance. The *Bretagne* began its trip back to Europe and stopped at each port in reverse order. After French officials said he was not welcome there, his last hope was his starting point: Italy. They, too, denied him.

Was O'Brien destined to once again be stuck sailing from port to port, never to touch *terra firma* again?

Good news arrived from a very unlikely source on October 12, 1953. *Parade Magazine*, the weekly magazine supplement found in Sunday newspapers across the United States, had taken up O'Brien's cause and arranged for him to live in the Dominican Republic. Eight days later, the *Bretagne* once again docked in Brazil, but this time O'Brien was permitted to disembark from the ship and dine with his estranged wife.

When O'Brien's plane touched down in Santo Domingo on October 27, 1953, he was finally allowed to walk free. In a November 29, 1953, interview with *Parade*, he stated, "So you want to know what it feels like to be a man without a country, huh? Okay, I'll tell you. It's like being a miserable old hound dog that gets kicked off every doorstep."

Inventor of the Other Teddy Bear

1940

When Theodore Bear died on November 19, 1940, newspapers noted that he was the inventor of the stuffed toy, the Teddy Bear. This, however, was incorrect. Teddy Bear was the inventor of another product known as the Teddy Bear, but it was not the well-known toy.

Bear was the owner of a garment manufacturing company named Theodore Bear, which produced clothing for infants, children, and women. To capitalize on the craze for the Teddy Bear stuffed toy, advertisements for the company featured an image of Theodore Bear's head superimposed on a stuffed bear.

When his firm designed a new women's undergarment that consisted of a top and bottom combined into a single piece, they decided to capitalize on his unique name. They coined this new garment the "Teddy Bear," commonly referred to as a Teddy today.

Because the company did not obtain design or patent protection, it wasn't long before other manufacturers began to market their own Teddies. Competition was tough and soon, Bear's business languished. On March 9, 1922, his creditors forced him into voluntary bankruptcy. "The creditors say Bear's assets will cover his liabilities in just about the same proportion as a 'Teddy Bear' covers its wearer—$33\frac{1}{3}$ per cent."

For Popular Prices See the Original

Line of Cloaks for Misses, Juniors Girls and Infants

On Display At Our Sample Rooms
22 So. Market Street.

As a special accommodation to visiting buyers during Style Show Week, we will open an annex sample room at the southeast corner of Market street and Jackson boulevard.

THEODORE BEAR

22 to 30 South Market Street   CHICAGO

July 17, 1915 advertisement for Theodore Bear.

New York's Romeo and Juliet

1939

A story about two lovers who wished to marry over parental objections.

Between the years 1935 and 1938, debutante Eileen Jackson Herrick was a steady feature of society and gossip columns in and around New York City. And there was good reason for this: the dark-haired, blue-eyed, curvaceous young woman looked great on the printed page, which indirectly helped sell more newspapers. Whether Herrick was at the beach in a sexy swimsuit, donning the latest fashion at a charity ball, or simply out-and-about with friends, a photographer was certain to snap her picture.

Herrick was born on August 4, 1919, to Mary Douglas Bosworth and Walter Richmond Herrick, a well-known New York City lawyer and former Manhattan park commissioner. Both of her parents were listed in the New York social register, which provided young Eileen entry into the upper echelon of New York society.

Perhaps the greatest advantage of being a celebutante is their ability to attract attention. Young male suitors were never in short supply and movie scouts hounded Herrick for screen tests. While it was likely little more than an unsubstantiated tabloid rumor, some claimed that Howard Hughes had taken a keen interest in her. But not all attention is good. In February of 1938, Herrick began receiving threatening letters, and her father responded by hiring a bodyguard to accompany her whenever she ventured out in public.

Eileen Herrick's life would forever change one day in the fall of 1938. While attending a cocktail party with one of her girlfriends, she spotted a man named George Lowther III. She had seen him previously at similar functions, but they had never formally met. Nineteen-year-old Herrick asked her friend to introduce her to thirty-year-old Lowther, and she graciously obliged. While it wasn't love at first sight, they began to date in December of 1938, and a romance soon blossomed.

Like Herrick, Lowther also came from a socially prominent family, though he himself had little monetary wealth. A graduate of Yale with an athletic physique, he was considered one of the most desirable of the young bachelors moving within Herrick's same social circles.

Fearing that news of their relationship would be met with disapproval from Herrick's parents, the two snuck around behind the their backs. Many times they would meet at friends' homes. When the couple needed some alone time, they would head off to remote beaches or simply take a ride in Lowther's car.

As the summer of 1939 approached, Herrick was faced with a tough decision: either spend summer at the family's vacation home in Wainscott, Long Island, or create an excuse to stay back in the city so that she could continue to see Lowther. She opted for the latter. Herrick initially accepted a position as a model in a dress shop, but soon secured a one-month position posing for photographs at one of the 1939 New York World's Fair automobile exhibits. This allowed her to stay in the city and visit Lowther during her time off.

Her plan seemed to be going smoothly until her father called the automobile company one day and learned that her modeling stint had ended three weeks prior. Her parents were furious and forbade her from ever seeing Lowther again. Herrick insisted that if they took the time to get to know him, they would withdraw their objections to the relationship.

One evening, Lowther was invited over to the Herrick townhouse at 148 East End Avenue in Manhattan, where her parents cornered him into a two-and-a-half-hour-long inquisition. At first the conversation was casual, but it wasn't long before Mrs. Herrick started her attack on Lowther. "If you believe that we don't care to have you go about with Eileen, you're right. We do object to you." From that moment on, she listed detail after detail on why he wasn't good enough for their daughter. At the end of the evening, Mrs. Herrick offered up the following proposal: If the two agreed not to see each other for six months and were still interested in marriage after that, the Herricks would withdraw the objections to their romance. The true motive of this suggestion was the hope that Herrick would lose interest in Lowther before then. The young couple, however, declined her parents' offer to stay apart.

In late August, shortly after this disastrous family meeting, Mrs. Herrick ordered Eileen to spend one month out at their summer home in Long Island so that she could take some time to think things over. Immediately upon arrival, Mrs. Herrick hid the car keys and had nurses and a private detective guarding Eileen day and night. She was now a virtual prisoner at Wainscott. Since autumn was setting in and the town was a summer resort, their nearest neighbors were over one-half mile (0.8 km) away. Eileen's only bits of allowed freedom were her walks along the empty beach with her black setter dog Gypsy.

While she wrote letters to Lowther every single day, nearly all were intercepted before they ever got to him.

Once her one-month sentence ended, Herrick and her parents returned to the city. One morning, while everyone was still asleep, she tiptoed down the stairs and right out the door. She left a note for her parents stating that she would be at her friend Helen Stedman's house at noon and would be spending the evening there. As soon as she arrived at Helen's house, Herrick telephoned Lowther and the two arranged to meet at the home of one of his friends. He took notice of the visible toll on Herrick's health that her parents' actions had taken, and the two determined that it was time to marry. Upon her return to the Stedman house later that day, Herrick was informed that her father had called and spoken to Helen's mother. Mrs. Stedman spoke the truth when she stated that she had no idea where Herrick was. In response, Mr. Herrick declared that he would be calling the Missing Persons Bureau to begin a search for his daughter.

Herrick's next move was to pen the following note and have it notarized: "I, Eileen Herrick am going to the Barbizon Hotel for woman [sic] November 7th 1939 to talk to my Mother or Father or both and I was kept before in Wainscott L. I. at our home by force and the reason was to keep me from seeing George Lowther III. As I am afraid of what might happen, I am writing this therefor [sic] to state that he George Lowther III did not force me to leave my family's house or to stay away or to do anything that my family might object to or disapprove of." She handed the note to Lowther before calling her mother to let her know where she was.

It wasn't long before two detectives arrived at the Barbizon and coaxed Eileen back to the Herrick townhouse. Once again, nurses watched over her night and day, and hired detectives listened in on every telephone call she attempted to make.

Lowther knew he needed to do something to get Herrick away from her parents. He consulted with his attorney Eli Johnson and told him, "I want to get her out of that house." Lowther continued, "I want to get her away before she has a nervous breakdown."

Johnson thought it best to sit down and talk with Mr. Herrick one-on-one before resorting to any form of legal action. Though their meeting lasted approximately two hours, they were unable to come to an agreement. Mr. Herrick was adamant on his opinion that George Lowther was not good enough for his daughter and reiterated the offer that the two lovebirds attempt a six-month separation.

It was on November 12, 1939, that the story broke in the news. Dubbed by the press as "Romeo and Juliet," it was reported that the couple planned to elope at 3:00 p.m. that day while Mr. Herrick was attending the meeting with attorney Eli Johnson. The story was so well-publicized that the Herricks were able to stop the elopement from occurring.

Attorney Johnson told Lowther there was only one legal move that could get Herrick out of her parents' home, and he had no idea if it would be successful. Using the notarized letter that Herrick had penned to Lowther while staying at the Barbizon as evidence, Johnson approached New York Supreme Court Justice Isidor Wasservogel and explained the facts to him. At 4:00 p.m. on November 13, 1939, Wasservogel signed a writ of habeas corpus demanding that Eileen appear before him the following day.

At nearly the same time that the writ was issued, Herrick's parents decided that she was suffering undue stress and felt it best to check her into the hospital to recover. Herrick was later quoted as stating, "I was taken to New York Hospital, a big institution near where we lived. But I did not understand that a writ had been served on father. Apparently this sending me away was an attempt to get me out of the reach of the law." She continued, "I was assigned to a large room, which seemed more cheerful than my own room at home. But I was constantly attended by nurses, and was not allowed to go anywhere alone. Nor was I permitted to have a telephone. I was completely cut off from the world, entirely unaware that a court battle had started that was to be the sensation of New York; a court battle over my love for George."

The hearing went on as scheduled. As the press filled the courthouse lobby, all those involved met in Judge Wasservogel's chamber at 2:30 p.m. All, that is, except for Eileen. The Herricks' attorney argued that she was too ill to appear in court, but the judge didn't buy any of it. He demanded that she be brought into the court to answer to the complaint that she was being held against her will. At 4:50 that afternoon, Mrs. Herrick arrived with a haggard-looking Eileen. Judge Wasservogel questioned Eileen as to whether she was being held against her will, how long she had been dating Lowther, and if she wished to marry him. In the end, he concluded that she was of legal age and free to make her own decisions. He ruled that the two needed to wait ten days—more than ample time for Herrick to recover from her supposed illness—and then they could marry.

This would prove to be a hollow victory. The Herricks were outraged by the judge's decision and determined to keep the young couple apart as long as possible. At first, George simply tried to call Eileen at the hospital, but doctor's orders prevented her from having access to a phone. Letters he wrote to her went unanswered. He attempted to send telegrams, but no one would sign for them. Judge Wasservogel was asked to intervene, but he said that he wouldn't take any action until the ten-day recovery period was over.

That was never to happen. On the eve of the end of their ten-day truce, one of Lowther's friends spotted a car with Herrick and her parents in it. He was able to tail the vehicle for a bit, but lost sight of it near Grand Central Station.

The hunt was now on for Eileen Herrick. No one was sure where her parents had taken her this time. Now that she was a national media sensation, newsmen followed up on every tip they received. Unfortunately, they all led nowhere. It was later learned that she had been staying in Asbury Park under an assumed name before being moved back to the family home in Wainscott. Once again guarded around the clock, Herrick took advantage of the fact that one of the bathrooms could be entered from both the hallway and the maid's room. She entered the bathroom, crossed over into the bedroom, stole some supplies, and penned a love letter to Lowther that warned him to stay away. It concluded with "Good-by, my sweet angel. I love you and always will, remember that. I'll go through hell for you, and I have. They'll never keep us apart, unless they kill me. All my love, my darling angel. E."

It's unclear who mailed the letter for Herrick, but upon receiving it, Lowther felt that drastic action needed to be taken. He drove with a friend out to Wainscott with the intention of bringing her back to the city. Yet, the press had already beaten the two there and somehow convinced those guarding Herrick to let her be photographed on the balcony of the Wainscott home. When Lowther finally arrived, he was photographed looking up toward the now-empty balcony before being chased off the premises by detectives. The two photos were run side-by-side in newspapers as a play on the classic *Romeo and Juliet* balcony scene.

Once again, Lowther turned to the legal system for help. On December 7, Suffolk County Judge L. Baron Hill issued the following ruling after a three-hour, closed-door hearing: "Eileen Herrick is free to leave the home of her parents, but as long as she lives with her parents and is supported by them, she is under their control." Lowther told reporters, "I've got a date with Eileen at 12:30 p.m. tomorrow to decide everything."

With that ruling, Eileen Herrick was once again moved to a new location. In an interview with the *New York Daily News* on December 9, she stated, "I want to be left alone for a while to think this whole thing over quietly and calmly." She added, "If it hadn't been for family interference I probably would have been married to George by now." Herrick commented that she needed "two or three months to decide whether [she] want[ed] to marry him." It appeared that all her parents' hard work was starting to pay off—Juliet was beginning to have second thoughts about marrying her Romeo.

But the interview was all a ruse. Herrick and Lowther had secretly planned to marry, but needed a way to throw her parents off track. She figured that if she pretended to lose interest in George, her parents would drop their guard and the two could sneak off together.

Everything initially went according to plan. The two went to a doctor and got their obligatory premarital blood tests. Certificates of health were issued for both, and they intended to elope the following morning. Then suddenly, on December

17, Herrick suffered an appendicitis attack and was rushed to the hospital for immediate surgery. She spent the next two weeks hospitalized and, because her parents were so convinced that her hot romance with Lowther had finally cooled off, they allowed her to have a phone in her room as a Christmas present. Herrick was able to talk to Lowther each day she remained in the hospital.

Upon her release, Herrick returned to her parents' home and, on the morning of January 4, 1940, told her parents that she felt well enough to take her dog for a walk. With Gypsy by her side, Herrick enjoyed her first few moments of unguarded freedom in months. She walked a total of three blocks to the corner of 2nd Avenue and East 86th Street and hailed a taxicab. Her destination? You guessed it—the loving arms of George Lowther III.

The two then hurried to Grand Central Station and boarded a train to New Haven, Connecticut. This was followed by a chartered flight to Portland, Maine. From there, the couple drove approximately sixty miles (nearly 100 km) northwest to the small town of North Conway, New Hampshire. In a small church, a young minister married the two on January 5, 1940.

Front and back of Eileen and George's marriage certificate. "Time waived and NY blood test accepted in lieu of NH by Judge of Probate" has been written in the margin.

Herrick told the press, "All I can say is that I am desperately happy to be with George at last, as I am sorry to have brought all this confusion and trouble to my friends. But all the worry is over now. I'm going to be one of the happiest and, I hope, one of the best wives anyone knows."

Lowther added, "I'm even happier than Eileen. I'm sorry we had all this trouble but it was worth it. I've got the best prize anyone could win. I'm upset that Eileen's parents don't like me, but I think they'll find in time that I'm the man who loves their daughter more than anyone else could, and that's saying a lot."

The Herricks, on the other hand, were less than pleased with the nuptials. "There's nothing we can do about the marriage," Mrs. Herrick stated. "We checked up and found it was perfectly legal." Mr. Herrick told reporters, "I know of no grounds to have it annulled. But if any of you gentlemen have any suggestions, I'd appreciate hearing them."

Four years later, the press caught up with the Lowthers and everything appeared to be going well. With the United States now embroiled in a World War, they picked up and moved to Beverly Hills. Eileen was learning to cook and do housework in the small apartment they rented, while George worked the night shift at a Lockheed Martin defense plant.

But the fairytale ending was not to be. One year later, on August 27, 1945, the couple legally separated. Their divorce was finalized on September 23, 1946.

George later remarried and raised a family out of the spotlight.

Eileen once again made headlines when she decided to marry Haitian Air Force Colonel Henry Wiener in 1952. Like her first marriage, this one also failed. Eileen wished to divorce Wiener and head back to New York with their young daughter Michelle, but Haitian law forbade her from taking the child out of the country. Her mental and physical health quickly deteriorated, and on the morning of January 1, 1955, Eileen passed away at thirty-five years of age. Her death certificate stated that the cause of death was a heart attack, but it was later reported in the press that friends had supplied her with sleeping tablets the previous evening. Eight tablets were found to be missing from the bottle. Unlike Shakespeare's Juliet, Eileen did not awaken from the poison she had taken. Eileen Herrick Wiener was buried in an above-ground white stone crypt that overlooked the Port au Prince harbor.

Sixty-Seven-Year-Old Has His First Birthday Party

1920

By all appearances, Joseph R. Smith had a full and rewarding life. He was a pioneer resident of Glen Ellyn, Illinois, the president of that village, and the president of the Glen Ellyn State Bank. Yet there was something he sorely missed: he'd never had a birthday party.

On Friday, January 24, 1920, Smith decided to make his dream come true. In honor of his sixty-seventh birthday, he held his own first birthday party at the Guild Hall in Glen Ellyn. Two hundred residents of Glen Ellyn were invited to celebrate with him. There was a birthday cake three feet (0.91 m) in diameter adorned with sixty-seven candles. A Chicago orchestra played as guests danced the night away.

"I never did have a party before and now that I've had my first I'm going to keep on having them. I'm going to make up for the sixty-odd I missed. A birthday party is a real sport. And I think, between you and me, the others got as much fun out of it as I did."

Mary Jane

2004

A personal story.

The fact that I did not marry until I was forty-five years of age would suggest that I was either a player or just really bad at dating. While every man would like to claim the former, I must admit that I fell in line with the latter. My self-perception was that I was a vertically challenged, shy geek with low self-esteem who didn't drink, smoke, or do drugs. Simply put, the dating scene was not the place for me.

It's not that I had never been in any serious long-term relationships. I dated some amazing women when I was younger, but for various reasons the relationships just never worked out. As I entered my thirties, I found myself in a world of happily married women who were raising families. The pool of eligible women seemed to dry up.

In the days before the World Wide Web, I tried the classified ads that were prominent in newspapers of the time. After reading about a newly launched service called Match.com in the mid-1990s, I signed up and, as a charter member, was granted a free membership that wouldn't expire until 2099. In the ten years that I used the service, I went out with a grand total of three women, all to no avail. I tried speed dating several times, but that also led nowhere. It became clear to me as I approached forty that I would most likely spend my life without a partner. It wasn't ideal, but I had gotten used to living alone, and that was okay.

Joe Nolette, however, had a different idea for my future. Joe was a student in a ninth grade Earth science class that I taught during the 2002–2003 school year. After he completed the course, Joe continued to show up in my classroom every couple of weeks to say hello (mainly to avoid going to his other classes). At some point during each conversation, Joe insisted that he was going to find the perfect woman for me.

In September of 2004, as Joe entered the eleventh grade, he walked into my room and stated, "I found the perfect woman for you." He said that he'd met her while attending a party at the home of his girlfriend's parents in Albany, New York. All Joe knew about this mystery woman was that she was a French teacher named Mary Jane, and he commented that he thought she was very pretty. My initial thought was that he was sixteen and his version of pretty was someone like *Baywatch* babe Pam Anderson. That was not my version of pretty. I jokingly told Joe to go away.

Joe did not listen well. The same basic conversation repeated itself every couple of weeks for the next two months. Then in early November, Joe once again walked into my room and handed me a small slip of paper with an email address on it. "I told her you'd contact her," he said. He was so confident we were a match that he added, "I want to be invited to the wedding."

Upon arriving home that evening, I set her email address aside and attempted to ignore it. Yet, every day I would give it a quick glance before moving on to something else. Two weeks later, I decided to send this mystery woman a message. I really didn't want to go out with her, but I felt an obligation to Joe and decided to go on a blind date with Mary Jane.

We decided to meet at the Spectrum Theater in Albany on Saturday, November 13, 2004. We had both agreed to wear red coats, and the only other physical detail I knew about Mary Jane was that she had blonde hair. As I stood in the theater lobby, I kept an eye out for her. Suddenly, a woman in red with blonde hair walked in, looked at me, and walked on by. I thought that maybe she looked at me and didn't like what she saw. I fidgeted as I continued to wait, and made my way outside when the lobby began to fill up.

I can only describe what happened next as being like a scene from a movie. As I stood under the bright lights of the theater marquee, snowflakes gently fell from the sky as an attractive blonde woman in a red coat slowly emerged from the darkness. Never was I more thankful to have listened to a student's advice. Mary Jane was indeed beautiful.

From my standpoint, that date was a disaster. First, we saw a movie titled *Vera Drake* about a woman who secretly performed abortions. Definitely not first date material. This was followed by a visit to a noisy bar a few blocks away. As someone who never consumes alcohol, I felt like a fish out of water. Yet, Mary Jane agreed to go out with me again. And again. And again...

In 2008 when Mary Jane and I decided to get married, Joe Nolette was the first person we invited. We had a small wedding where Joe gave a wonderful speech explaining why he thought we were perfect for each other. While he may not have been the world's best Earth science student, by introducing me to my wife, he forever changed my life for the better.

As I write these words, Mary Jane and I have been together for more than fifteen years. She has patiently allowed me the time and solitude needed to research and write this volume. For this reason and so many more that I could never put into words, this book is dedicated to my wife, Mary Jane Guidon.

April 2018 photograph of Mary Jane and the author.

SOURCES

This book represents a collection of stories that I have researched over a period of many years. It would be impossible for me to assemble a list of every source that was referenced, so I have opted for a more simplistic approach that violates all rules of proper citation. What you'll find below is a data dump from my computer's hard drive for each story. Stories are listed in order of the date that they occurred, not in the order that they appear in the book.

The source organization system I developed is preserved below: Year_Month_Day_Source_Page#. While story titles and author names are absent, this should provide enough information for anyone wishing to research these stories further.

Please note that the page numbers may not be accurate. For example, if an article originally appeared on page B-1 of a publication, the database in which I found the story may have had it listed on page 13. Also, since some newspapers had multiple daily editions, a story that appeared on page 4 of a particular edition may be listed in the archives as page 132.

Images for the book are courtesy of: NYC Municipal Archives ("The Green Parrot Murder"); State Archives of Florida ("A Date with Death" and "The Flying Bandits"); University of California, Los Angeles, Library Special Collections ("She Dared to Wear Slacks"); John Murphy ("The Salem Trade School Football Team"); M.H.A. ("Two Weeks on Venus"); Gary Silverman ("The Crayola Caper" and "Mary Jane"); US Naval History and Heritage Command ("Beached Steel"); Minnesota

Historical Society ("The Last Man Standing"); patents and public domain; and the author.

The Rescue of Charles Nalle (1860)

I highly recommend the book *Freeing Charles* by Scott Christianson (2010, University of Illinois Press). It is the most complete work on the life of Charles Nalle.

1860_04_28_Troy_Daily_Times_p2

1860_04_30_New_York_Morning_Express_p4

1860_04_30_Troy_Daily_Times_p2

1860_04_30_Troy_Daily_Times_p3

1860_05_01_Troy_Daily_Times_p2

1860_05_02_Troy_Daily_Times_p2

1860_05_02_Troy_Daily_Whig_p3

1860_05_02_Weekly_Anglo-African_p3

1860_05_03_Hudson_Weekly_Star_p2

1860_05_03_The_Sabbath_Recorder_p190

1860_05_03_Troy_Daily_Times_p2

1860_05_24_Troy_Daily_Times_p3

1860_05_30_Lockport_Journal_and_Courier_p2

1860_06_07_Troy_Daily_Times_p3

1860_07_19_Albany_Atlas_and_Argus_p3

1860_07_31_Daily_Union_p2

1860_08_02_Daily_Saratogian_p2

1860_08_06_Daily_Union_p2

1860_08_27_Daily_Saratogian_p2

1875_07_29_Daily_Saratogian_p2

1908_09_08_Troy_Times_p5

1911_06_08_New_York_Age_p8

1913_04_12_Cortland_Standard_p6

1932_08_10_Troy_Times_p5

1933_05_19_Troy_Times_p5

1933_05_20_Troy_Times_p6

1933_06_05_Troy_Times_p5

1941_05_06_Troy_Times_Record_p9

Beached Steel (1868)

1868_04_24_Indiana_Gazette_p1

1868_09_13_Memphis_Daily_Appeal_p2

1868_09_14_Harrisburg_Telegraph_p1

1877_05_31_Chicago_Tribune_p1

1919_08_15_Billings_Gazette_p4

The Wheelbarrow Man (1878)

1878_06_14_Muscatine_Daily_Journal_p4

1878_06_21_Quad-City_Times_p1

1878_07_08_Fort_Wayne_Sentinel_p4

1878_07_18_Fort_Wayne_Sentinel_p4

1878_07_23_Saint_Paul_Globe_p2

1878_07_24_Quad-City_Times_p4

1878_07_31_Black_Hills_Daily_Times_p4

1878_08_01_Black_Hills_Daily_Times_p4

1878_08_07_Fort_Wayne_Sentinel_p4

1878_08_15_Fort_Wayne_Sentinel_p4

1878_08_21_Hawaiian_Gazette_p3

1878_08_26_Buffalo_Commercial_p3

1878_08_28_Des_Moines_Register_p2

1878_09_20_Nevada_State_Journal_p3

1878_09_24_The_Times_p2

1878_09_27_Reno_Gazette-Journal_p3

1878_10_12_Placer_Herald_p5

1878_10_15_San_Francisco_Examiner_p2

1878_10_16_Boston_Post_p2

1878_10_17_Inter_Ocean_p2

1878_10_26_New_Orleans_Weekly_Democrat_p5

1878_10_28_New_York_Daily_Herald_p7

1878_10_29_Reno_Gazette-Journal_p1

1878_10_31_Weekly_Davenport_Democrat_p3

1878_11_06_Oakland_Tribune_p1

1878_11_07_Cincinnati_Enquirer_p2

1878_11_12_Reno_Gazette-Journal_p1

1878_11_15_True_Northerner_p7

1878_11_20_San_Francisco_Chronicle_p3

1878_11_26_San_Francisco_Chronicle_p3

1879_02_04_Nevada_State_Journal_p3

1879_03_01_Daily_Ogden_Junction_p4

1879_03_10_Philadelphia_Times_p2

1879_03_15_Buffalo_Express_p4

1879_03_28_Hays_City_Sentinel_p3

1879_03-13_Des_Moines_Register_p3

1879_04_03_Russell_Record_p3

1879_04_04_Hays_City_Sentinel_p3

1879_04_14_Omaha_Daily_Bee_p2

1879_04_15_Philadephia_Times_p2

1879_05_14_Pantagraph_p1

1879_05_27_Cincinnati_Daily_Star_p4

1879_05_28_Huntsville_Weekly_Democrat_p1

1879_06_11_Wilmington_News-Journal_p3

1879_06_18_Pittsburgh_Daily_Post_p4

1879_06_24_Lawrence_Daily_Journal_p4

1879_06_26_Altoona_Tribune_p3

1879_06_28_Junction_City_Weekly_Union_p1

1879_06_29_Philadelphia_Times_p4

1879_07_09_Arkansas_Democrat_p3

1879_07_25_Brooklyn_Daily_Eagle_p2

1879_07_25_New_York_Daily_Herald_p9

1879_07_31_Daily_Register_p3

1879_08_28_St_Louis_Globe-Democrat_p4

1880_01_17_Cincinnati_Daily_Star_p1

1880_07_07_Pittsburgh_Daily_Post_p4

1880_09_05_Tennessean_p3

1880_09_28_Bedford_Press_p3

1880_11_19_Wilmington_Morning_News_p3

1880_12_17_Wilson_Advance_p4

1881_05_19_National_Republican_p4

1881_12_02_Charlotte_Democrat_p1

1883_04_05_Carolina_Watchman_p3

1883_04_05_Chatham_Record_p2

1883_04_30_New_York_Times_p2

1883_05_06_Detroit_Free_Press_p18

1883_09_22_York_Daily_p3

The Last Man Standing (1885)

1918_08_08_Washington_Post_p4

1923_07_22_Chicago_Daily_Tribune_p9

1923_07_22_Los_Angeles_Times_pI-2

1923_07_22_New_York_Times_p24

1924_07_22_New_York_Times_p15

1925_07_22_New_York_Times_p5

1926_07_22_New_York_Times_p4

1926_07_23_Hartford_Courant_p5

1927_07_22_Chicago_Daily_Tribune_p1

1927_07_22_Los_Angeles_Times_p2

1927_07_22_Washington_Post_p2

1927_07_23_Los_Angeles_Times_p2

1928_07_22_New_York_Times_p35

1929_07_17_Los_Angeles_Times_p7

1929_07_17_New_York_Times_p18

1929_08_29_New_York_Times_p15

1930_04_19_New_York_Times_p13

1930_04_23_Chicago_Daily_Tribune_p9

1930_07_20_New_York_Times_p18

1930_07_22_New_York_Times_p15

1931_05_07_Boston_Globe_p14

1931_05_08_New_York_Times_p27

1931_05_09_New_York_Times_p3

1931_06_19_New_York_Times_p29

1931_07_22_Minneapolis_Star_Tribune_p9

1932_01_17_Los_Angeles_Times_p1

1932_07_17_Washington_Post_p11

1932_07_22_New_York_Times_p17

1933_07_22_New_York_Times_p6

1935_08_17_Chicago_Tribune_p18

1935_10_05_Albert_Lea_Evening_Tribune_p1

1935_10_05_Bismark_Tribune_p3

1935_10_05_Logansport_Pharos_Tribune_p5

1939_05_22_Gettysburg_Times_p4

A King without a Country (1893)

1880_08_13_Baltimore_Sun_p4

1880_09_02_Chicago_Tribune_p4

1887_04_21_Times-Picayune_p2

1887_04_24_Richmond_Dispatch_p2

1887_04_28_San_Francisco_Chronicle_p6

1890_11_06_Evening_Republic_p3

1893_11_05_New-York_Tribune_p1

1894_06_23_New_York_Times_p23

1895_03_15_Kansas_Semi-Weekly_Capital_p7

1895_06_18_New_York_Times_p3

1895_06_27_Pottsville_Republican_p3

1895_07_01_Los_Angeles_Herald_p4

1895_07_03_Los_Angeles_Herald_p1

1895_07_26_New_York_Times_p1

1895_08_01_New_York_Times_p1

1895_08_02_Los_Angeles_Times_p3

1895_08_06_New_York_Times_p4

1895_08_07_New_York_Times_p1

1895_08_09_New_York_Times_p5

1895_08_18_New_York_Times_p2

1895_10_04_New_York_Times_p1

1895_10_06_Los_Angeles_Times_p22

1898_02_01_New_York_Times_p1

1898_02_11_Los_Angeles_Times_p1

1898_02_11_Los_Angeles_Times_p2

1898_02_13_New_York_Times_p1

1907_08_06_New_York_Times_p1

1908_12_19_The_Wasp_p9

1924_11_09_Los_Angeles_Times_p31

1925_11_02_Hartford_Courant_p9

1926_01_11_Boston_Globe_p9

1946_12_Smash_Comics_p42

Educated Women Are Unfit as Wives (1904)
1904_06_08_Chicago_Daily_Tribune_p4

Falling Girl Saved by Spike (1911)
1911_03_28_ Ottumwa_Tri-Weekly_Courier_p8

1911_06_17_Honolulu_Evening_Bulletin_p6

1911_12_13_New_York_Evening_World_p4

Man Inherits Fortune from Woman He Never Met (1912)
1912_03_04_St_Louis_Dispatch_p14

1912_03_26_Brooklyn_Citizen_p1

1912_06_01_Brooklyn_Daily_Eagle_p18

1912_06_02_Brooklyn_Daily_Eagle_p8

1912_06_03_Brooklyn_Daily_Eagle_p20

Sues for Canary's Lost Love (1917)

1917_12_30_New_York_Sun_p17

1918_01_01_Independence_Daily_Reporter_p4

Sixty-Seven-Year-Old Has His First Birthday Party (1920)

1920_01_25_Chicago_Daily_Tribune_p12

1927_05_19_McHenry_Plaindealer_p4

Arrested for Eating Soup Loudly (1923)

1923_12_15_New_York_Sun_p1

1923_12_14_Indiana_Weekly_Messenger_p12

An Unusual Chicken Thief (1925)

1925_07_01_Elmira_Star_Gazette_p13

1925_09_22_Star_Gazette_p16

1925_10_02_Elmira_Star_Gazette_p29

The Average Man (1927)

1927_10_19_Mount_Carmel_Daily_Republican-Register_p2

1927_10_19_Muscatine_Journal_p9

1927_10_19_St_Petersburg_Times_p4

1927_10_20_Los_Angeles_Times_p5

1927_10_21_Davenport_Daily_Times_p2

1927_10_21_Oshkosh_Northwestern_p14

1927_10_22_Akron_Beacon_Journal_p1

1927_10_22_Lancaster_News_Journal_p2

1927_10_22_Los_Angeles_Times_p3

1927_10_22_Sioux_City_Journal_p9

1927_10_22_Stevens_Point_Daily_p1

1927_10_22_Washington_Post_p1

1927_10_23_Sioux_City_Journal_p1

1927_10_27_Des_Moines_Register_p3

1927_10_28_Des_Moines_Tribune_p13

1927_11_06_Des_Moines_Register_p29

1927_11_06_Des_Moines_Register_p68

1927_11_09_Daily_Mountain_Eagle_p9

1928_10_23_Des_Moines_Tribune_p7

1928_12_10_Cedar_Rapids_Evening_Gazette_and_
Republican_p5

1929_10_20_Washington_Post_pM17

1930_01_05_Burlington_Hawk-Eye_Gazette_p5

1930_07_08_Hartford_Courant_p13

1930_07_27_Los_Angeles_Times_pA4

1932_03_20_Cedar_Rapids_Sunday_Gazette_and_
Republican_p4

1934_04_23_Des_Moines_Tribune_p7

1935_03_01_Muscatine_Journal_p6

1935_04_05_Mason_City_Globe-Gazette_p2

1935_04_23_New_York_Times_p23

1935_04_23_Washington_Post_p11

1936_10_25_Des_Moines_Register_p26

The Salem Trade School Football Team (1929)

1926_09_17_Boston_Daily_Globe_p21

1926_09_19_Boston_Daily_Globe_pB-21

1928_10_06_Boston_Daily_Globe_p7

1928_10_30_Daily_Boston_Globe_p27

1928_11_09_Portsmouth_Herald_p1

1929_09_22_Daily_Boston_Globe_pA-23

1929_09_29_Daily_Boston_Globe_pA-24

1929_10_13_Daily_Boston_Globe_p16

1929_10_16_Boston_Globe_p2

1929_10_17_Daily_Boston_Globe_p16

1929_10_17_Daily_Boston_Globe_p16a

1929_10_17_New_York_Times_p42

1929_10_17_Oakland_Tribune_p30

1929_10_18_Daily_Boston_Globe_p26

1929_10_18_Daily_Boston_Globe_p35

1929_10_18_Newport_Mercury_and_Weekly_News_p5

1929_10_19_Daily_Boston_Globe_p6

1929_10_19_Moorhead_Daily_News_p10

1929_10_23_Daily_Boston_Globe_p18

1929_11_12_Lowell_Sun_p36

1929_11_15_Daily_Boston_Globe_p41

1929_11_16_Lewiston_Daily_Sun_p14

1929_11_22_Daily_Boston_Globe_p29

1929_11_23_Daily_Boston_Globe_p3

1929_11_24_Daily_Boston_Globe_pA30

1929_11_27_Concord_Enterprise_p16

1929_12_14_Old_Gold_and_Black_p1

1929_12_14_Old_Gold_and_Black_p4

1930_01_08_Daily_Boston_Globe_p22

1930_09_21_Daily_Boston_Globe_p29

1930_10_27_Daily_Boston_Globe_p8

1930_11_03_Daily_Boston_Globe_p9

1930_11_12_Daily_Boston_Globe_p15

1930_11_17_Daily_Boston_Globe_p9

1931_09_21_Daily_Boston_Globe_p8

1936_09_30_Daily_Boston_Globe_p27

1937_11_10_Portsmouth_Herald_and_Times_p8

1959_10_22_Daily_Boston_Globe_p37

1972_06_25_Boston_Globe_p74

1972_06_28_Newport_Daily_News_p18

1989_09_12_Boston_Globe_p34

1995_11_05_Boston_Globe_p26

The Womanless Library (1930)

1930_02_07_Le_Mars_Semi-Weekly_Sentinel_p1

1930_09_08_Le_Mars_Globe-Post_p10

1930_09_09_Le_Mars_Semi-Weekly_Sentinel_p1

1930_09_12_Le_Mars_Semi-Weekly_Sentinel_p1

1930_09_15_Le_Mars_Globe-Post_p1

1930_09_15_Le_Mars_Globe-Post_p4

1930_09_16_Le_Mars_Semi-Weekly_Sentinel_p1

1930_09_18_Le_Mars_Globe-Post_p1

1930_09_19_Chicago_Daily_Tribune_p21

1930_09_19_Le_Mars_Semi-Weekly_Sentinel_p1

1930_09_19_Los_Angeles_Times_p1

1930_09_19_New_York_Times_p1

1930_09_19_Oelwein_Daily_Register_p1

1930_09_21_Hartford_Courant_p8

1930_09_22_Le_Mars_Globe-Post_p3

1930_09_23_Le_Mars_Semi-Weekly_Sentinel_p1

1930_09_25_Hawarden_Independent_p14

1930_09_25_Le_Mars_Globe-Post_p1

1930_09_29_Le_Mars_Globe-Post_p6

1930_09_29_Le_Mars_Semi-Weekly_Sentinel_p1

1930_10_02_Terril_Record_p4

1930_10_07_Hartford_Courant_p14

1930_10_16_Le_Mars_Globe-Post_p1

1930_10_17_Le_Mars_Semi-Weekly_Sentinel_p1

1930_10_17_Mason_City_Globe_Gazette_p1

1930_11_20_Le_Mars_Globe-Post_p1

1930_11_23_Arizona_Daily_Star_p32

1930_11_23_Los_Angeles_Times_pK-18

1930_11_27_Los_Angeles_Times_pA-9

1931_01_12_Le_Mars_Globe-Post_p1

1931_02_09_Le_Mars_Globe-Post_p1

1931_02_26_Le_Mars_Globe-Post_p1

1931_03_07_Oelwein_Daily_Register_p1

1931_03_09_Le_Mars_Globe-Post_p1

1931_03_10_Le_Mars_Semi-Weekly_Sentinel_p1

1931_03_12_Le_Mars_Globe-Post_p3

1931_03_31_Le_Mars_Semi-Weekly_Sentinel_p5

1931_04_20_Le_Mars_Globe-Post_p1

1931_07_02_Le_Mars_Globe-Post_p1

1931_07_03_Ames_Daily_Tribune_Times_p2

1931_07_07_Le_Mars_Semi-Weekly_Sentinel_p1

1931_07_10_Alton_Democrat_p1

1931_09_14_Le_Mars_Globe-Post_p5

1931_11_06_Le_Mars_Semi-Weekly_Sentinel_p1

1931_12_28_Le_Mars_Globe-Post_p1

1932_01_07_Terril_Record_p1

1932_01_07_Terril_Record_p2

1932_02_11_Akron_Register_Tribune_p4

1932_03_10_Ames_Daily_Tribune_Times_p8

1932_03_11_Le_Mars_Semi-Weekly_Sentinel_p1

1932_03_17_Emmetsburg_Democrat_p6

1932_03_29_Le_Mars_Semi-Weekly_Sentinel_p1

1932_04_12_Le_Mars_Semi-Weekly_Sentinel_p1

1932_04_15_Le_Mars_Semi-Weekly_Sentinel_p1

1932_05_20_Le_Mars_Semi-Weekly_Sentinel_p1

1932_05_24_Oelwein_Daily_Register_p8

1932_09_22_Le_Mars_Globe-Post_p1

1932_11_24_Hawarden_Independent_p11

1932_12_11_Fort_Madison_Evening_Democrat_p8

1932_12_15_Akron_Register_Tribune_p1

1933_03_28_Huron_Evening_Huronite_p10

1933_03_31_Le_Mars_Semi-Weekly_Sentinel_p1

1933_04_07_Le_Mars_Semi-Weekly_Sentinel_p1

1933_04_17_Moberly_Monitor_Index_p7

1933_04_18_Burlington_Gazette_p1

1933_04_18_Burlington_Hawk_Eye_p1

1933_04_18_Waterloo_Daily_Courier_p1

1933_04_19_Burlington_Hawk_Eye_p2

1933_04_20_Akron_Register_Tribune_p1

1933_04_21_Le_Mars_Semi-Weekly_Sentinel_p1

1933_04_25_Fort_Madison_Evening_Democrat_p8

1933_04_28_Burlington_Gazette_p1

1933_04_28_Mount_Pleasant_News_p1

1933_04_29_Burlington_Gazette_p1

1933_04_29_Huntington_Daily_News_p1

1933_04_29_New_York_Herald_Tribune_p1

1933_04_29_Syracuse_Herald_p1

1933_05_03_New_York_Times_p8

1933_05_04_Carroll_Daily_Herald_p1

1933_05_04_Toronto_Globe_p2

1933_05_04_Waterloo_Daily_Courier_p5

1933_05_07_Des_Moines_Register_p24

1933_05_08_Washington_Post_p2

1933_05_11_Washington_Post_p2

1933_06_01_Mason_City_Globe_Gazette_p1

1933_07_28_Lincoln_Nebraska_State_Journal_p1

1933_08_29_Le_Mars_Semi-Weekly_Sentinel_p1

1933_09_08_Le_Mars_Semi-Weekly_Sentinel_p8

1933_09_19_Fresno_Bee_p5

1933_10_31_Le_Mars_Semi-Weekly_Sentinel_p1

1935_01_10_Le_Mars_Globe-Post_p1

1937_05_18_Le_Mars_Semi-Weekly_p1

1940_10_08_Le_Mars_Semi-Weekly_p1

1940_10_10_Hawarden_Independent_p13

Fed a Yak at Midnight (1935)

1935_07_03_New_York_Times_p19

Can't Take It Anymore (1936)

1928_05_21_Tulare_Advance-Register_p1

1936_05_17_Los_Angeles_Times_p14

1936_05_18_San_Francisco_Examiner_p5

1936_06_12_San_Bernardino_County_Sun_p25

1936_06_22_Oakland_Tribune_p17

1975_09_18_Rayne_Acadian_Tribune_p30

Jerry the Mule Facing Execution (1936)

1936_06_22_Los_Angeles_Times_p22

1936_07_14_Los_Angeles_Times_p20

A Date with Death (1938)

1938_02_16_Orlando_Evening_Star_p1

1938_02_17_Orlando_Evening_Star_p1

1938_02_17_Orlando_Sentinel_p1

1938_02_18_Orlando_Evening_Star_p1

1938_02_18_Orlando_Sentinel_p1

1938_02_20_Orlando_Evening_Star_p1

1938_02_20_Orlando_Evening_Star_p1-a

1938_02_22_Orlando_Evening_Star_p1

1938_02_24_Orlando_Evening_Star_p1

1938_02_25_Orlando_Sentinel_p1

1938_03_23_Orlando_Evening_Star_p2

1938_03_30_Orlando_Sentinel_p12

1938_03_31_Orlando_Evening_Star_p1

1938_03_31_Orlando_Sentinel_p1

1938_04_02_Orlando_Sentinel_p3

1938_04_28_Orlando_Sentinel_p12

1938_05_01_Orlando_Evening_Star_p23

1938_05_02_Orlando_Sentinel_p1

1938_05_03_Orlando_Sentinel_p1

1938_05_04_Orlando_Evening_Star_p1

1938_05_04_Orlando_Evening_Star_p2

1938_05_06_Orlando_Evening_Star_p1

1938_05_06_Orlando_Sentinel_p1

1938_05_14_Orlando_Evening_Star_p1

1938_05_17_Orlando_Sentinel_p8

1938_07_20_Orlando_Sentinel_p9

1939_02_09_Orlando_Sentinel_p2

1939_02_26_Orlando_Sentinel_p6

1939_05_14_Orlando_Evening_Star_p7

1939_05_19_Orlando_Evening_Star_p1

1939_07_07_Orlando_Sentinel_p11

1939_07_15_Orlando_Sentinel_p1

1939_11_13_Orlando_Evening_Star_p1

1939_11_16_Orlando_Sentinel_p2

1939_11_17_Orlando_Sentinel_p4

1939_11_18_Orlando_Evening_Star_p1

1939_11_18_Orlando_Sentinel_p1

1940_02_26_Orlando_Sentinel_p3

1940_02_28_Orlando_Sentinel_p1

1940_03_01_Orlando_Sentinel_p1

1940_03_02_Orlando_Sentinel_p2

1940_03_09_Orlando_Sentinel_p1

1940_03_14_Orlando_Sentinel_p3

1940_03_19_Orlando_Sentinel_p2

1940_11_24_Orlando_Sentinel_p1

1942_10_10_Tampa_Tribune_p14

1952_01_06_Orlando_Sentinel_p35

1954_06_20_Orlando_Sentinel_p39

1959_05_31_Orlando_Sentinel_p33-F

1965_10_31_Orlando_Sentinel_p7-F

1993_06_20_Orlando_Sentinel_pK-2

The Search for Lucinda Trow (1938)

1938_02_08_Le_Mars_Semi-Weekly_Sentinel_p1

1938_11_10_Le_Mars_Globe-Post_p1

1938_11_13_Helena_Independent_p16

1938_11_14_Le_Mars_Globe-Post_p1

1938_11_15_Le_Mars_Semi-Weekly_Sentinel_p1

1938_11_15_Le_Mars_Semi-Weekly_Sentinel_p1-a

1938_11_17_Le_Mars_Globe-Post_p1

1938_11_21_Le_Mars_Globe-Post_p1

1938_11_22_Le_Mars_Semi-Weekly_Sentinel_p1

1938_12_01_Hammond_Times_p1

1938_12_02_Oelwein_Daily_Register_p2

1938_12_05_Le_Mars_Globe-Post_p1

1938_12_08_Hawarden_Independent_p3

1939_01_13_Le_Mars_Semi-Weekly_Sentinel_p1

1939_08_10_Le_Mars_Globe-Post_p1

1939_08_11_Mason_City_Globe_Gazette_p2

1941_03_13_Sioux_Center_News_p10

1941_07_18_Le_Mars_Semi-Weekly_Sentinel_p1

1972_02_14_Le_Mars_Daily_Sentinel_p4

1972_02_21_Le_Mars_Daily_Sentinel_p5

1993_08_04_Le_Mars_Daily_Sentinel_p11

She Dared to Wear Slacks (1938)

1938_11_10_Los_Angeles_Times_pA1

1938_11_11_San_Bernardino_County_Sun_p4

1938_11_15_Chicago_Daily_Tribune_p1

1938_11_15_Los_Angeles_Times_pA-8

1938_11_16_Chicago_Daily_Tribune_p1

1938_11_16_Harrisburg_Evening_News_p3

1938_11_16_Hartford_Courant_p1

1938_11_16_Los_Angeles_Times_pA1

1938_11_16_New_York_Daily_News_p4

1938_11_17_Los_Angeles_Times_pA-8

1938_11_18_Los_Angeles_Times_pA-3

1938_11_18_Oakland_Tribune_p1

1938_11_19_Los_Angeles_Times_pA-1

1938_11_21_Los_Angeles_Times_pA-4

1938_12_24_Los_Angeles_Times_pA-1

1939_01_08_Salt_Lake_Tribune_p54

1939_01_18_Daily_Hawk_Eye_Gazette_p1

1939_01_18_Harrisburg_Telegraph_p2

1939_01_18_Los_Angeles_Times_pA-3

1990_04_14_Pittsburgh_Gazette_p6

2014_10_24_Los_Angeles_Times

Husband's Life Is Saved by Wife's Thigh (1939)

1939_04_13_Bakersfield_Californian_p14

1939_04_14_Austin_Statesman_p10

New York's Romeo and Juliet (1939)

1926_04_14_The_Tennessean_p12

1935_07_13_New_York_Daily_News_p14

1935_07_14_New_York_Daily_News_p35

1935_08_11_Brooklyn_Daily_Eagle_p13

1937_08_17_Akron_Beacon_Journal_p17

1937_09_22_New_York_Daily_News_p25

1937_12_05_New_York_Daily_News_p54

1938_01_17_New_York_Daily_News_p37

1938_01_29_New_York_Daily_News_p9

1938_02_21_Wilkes-Barre_Times_Leader_p20

1938_02_24_Austin_American-Statesman_p3

1938_02_25_New_York_Daily_News_p30

1938_02_26_Ithaca_Journal_p4

1938_08_30_New_York_Daily_News_p4

1938_09_05_New_York_Daily_News_p2

1939_05_19_Ithaca_Journal_p10

1939_11_11_New_York_Daily_News_p2

1939_11_12_New_York_Daily_News_p4

1939_11_13_New_York_Daily_News_p2

1939_11_14_New_York_Daily_News_p4

1939_11_15_Democrat_and_Chronicle_p4

1939_11_16_New_York_Daily_News_p3

1939_11_17_New_York_Daily_News_p3

1939_11_19_Brooklyn_Daily_Eagle_p28

1939_11_23_New_York_Daily_News_pM-36

1939_11_25_New_York_Daily_News_p4

1939_11_27_New_York_Daily_News_p3

1939_11_28_New_York_Daily_News_p21

1939_11_30_New_York_Daily_News_p6

1939_12_01_New_York_Daily_News_p4

1939_12_02_Star-Gazette_p1

1939_12_08_New_York_Daily_News_p2

1939_12_09_New_York_Daily_News_p5

1939_12_10_New_York_Daily_News_p4

1939_12_10_New_York_Daily_News_pC-2

1939_12_27_New_York_Daily_News_pM-32

1940_01_05_New_York_Daily_News_p3

1940_01_06_New_York_Daily_News_p3

1940_01_07_New_York_Daily_News_p3

1940_01_08_New_York_Daily_News_p4

1940_01_14_New_York_Daily_News_p3

1940_01_20_New_York_Daily_News_p36

1940_02_05_Brooklyn_Daily_Eagle_p19

1940_03_25_New_York_Daily_News_p1

1940_03_29_New_York_Daily_News_p63

1940_05_True_Story_p22

1940_06_True_Story_p34

1944_05_21_New_York_Daily_News_p46

1946_09_07_New_York_Daily_News_p4

1946_09_24_New_York_Daily_News_p29

1952_12_02_San_Francisco_Examiner_p20

1953_07_22_Albany_Times-Union_p24

1954_07_30_Star-Gazette_p10

1955_01_06_East_Hampton_Star_p4

1955_03_06_New_York_Daily_News_p3

1955_03_06_New_York_Daily_News_pC-3

1955_10_27_Record-Argus_p11

Inventor of the Other Teddy Bear (1940)

1922_03_10_Los_Angeles_Times_pI-1

Woman Bites Dog (1941)

1941_11_06_Santa_Cruz_Evening_News_p1

1942_01_26_Shamokin_News_Dispatch_p6

The Green Parrot Murder (1942)

1922_08_02_The_Tennessean_p5

1942_07_13_New_York_Daily_News_p

1943_11_06_Baltimore_Evening_Sun_p16

1943_11_06_Camden_Evening_Courier_p3

1943_11_06_Chicago_Tribune_p1

1943_11_06_New_York_Daily_News_p5

1943_11_06_New_York_Times_p28

1943_11_06_Troy_Record_p1

1943_11_13_New_York_Amsterdam_News_p1-A

The Strange Case of the Jitterbug Coal (1944)

1944_04_13_Bismarck_Tribune_p4

1944_04_13_Columbus_Telegram_p1

1944_04_14_Bismarck_Tribune_p3

1944_04_14_Hartford_Courant_p18

1944_04_15_Bismarck_Tribune_p3

1944_04_15_Lead_Daily_Call_p1

1944_04_15_Washington_Post_p3

1944_04_16_Los_Angeles_Times_p11

1944_04_17_Bismarck_Tribune_p1

1944_04_18_Bismarck_Tribune_p1

The Los Angeles Perfume Bombing (1948)

1948_02_09_Neenah_News-Record_p1

1948_02_10_Hartford_Courant_p1

1948_02_11_Daily_Oklahoman_p9

1948_02_11_St_Joseph_News-Press_p1

1948_02_12_Democrat_and_Chronicle_p8

1948_02_12_Hartford_Courant_p10

1948_02_13_Casa_Grande_Dispatch_p6

1948_02_13_Lancaster_Eagle-Gazette_p6

1948_03_11_Syracuse_Post-Standard_p7

1948_03_19_Syracuse_Post-Standard_p12

1948_09_13_Los_Angeles_Times_p4

1948_09_13_Valley_Morning_Star_p5

1948_09_14_Gastonia_Gazette_p7

1948_09_14_Los_Angeles_Times_p2

1948_09_14_Sheboygan_Press_p1

1948_09_16_Vancouver_Sun_p9

1950_12_04_Life_p129

1950_12_13_Muster_Times_p26

1953_06_26_St_Louis_Post-Dispatch_p1-D

1953_07_01_Logan_Daily_News_p16

1957_10_27_Hartford_Courant_p97

1958_05_04_Hartford_Courant_p4-F

1959_05_24_Bridgeport_Post_pA-16

1959_07_10_London_Guardian_p1

1959_07_11_Sydney_Morning_Herald_p3

1959_07_15_Miami_News_p2-A

1959_12_10_St_Louis_Post-Dispatch_p3-F

1963_01_21_Bridgeport_Post_p1

Tender Young Alice, They Say (1949)

1949_04_14_Evening_Journal_p10

1949_04_14_Pittsburgh_Press_p9

1949_04_14_Toledo_Blade_p1

1949_04_15_El_Paso_Times_p20

1949_04_15_Odessa_American_p1

1949_04_15_Press_and_Sun-Bulletin_p1

1949_04_15_Traverse_City_Record_Eagle_p2

1949_04_15_Valley_Morning_Star_p16

1949_04_16_Galveston_News_p6

1949_04_16_Valparaiso_Vidette_Messenger_p7

1949_04_16_Washington_Post_p1

1949_04_17_Galveston_Daily_News_p9

1949_04_18_Evening_Journal_p2

1949_04_18_Galveston_Daily_News_p3

1949_04_18_Racine_Journal_Times_p8

1949_08_23_Austin_American-Statesman_p19

One-a-Day Triplets (1950)

1950_03_10_Chicago_Tribune_p1

1950_04_01_Weekly_Town_Hall_p2

1950_05_19_Eunice_News_p20

1951_03_08_Shreveport_Times_p15

1964_06_14_Shreveport_Times_p6-F

Ferryboat O'Brien (1952)

1926_09_23_Klamath_News_p6

1952_10_05_Washington_Post_pM-4

1952_10_18_Chicago_Daily_Tribune_p16

1952_10_20_Life_p34

1952_11_10_Chicago_Tribune_pC-2

1952_11_17_Chicago_Tribune_p13

1952_11_19_Chicago_Tribune_p6

1952_11_20_Chicago_Tribune_p2

1952_12_19_Hartford_Courant_p26-D

1952_12_26_Hartford_Courant_15-A

1952_12_31_Los_Angeles_Times_p12

1953_01_02_Chicago_Tribune_p7

1953_01_07_Los_Angeles_Times_p12

1953_03_08_Baltimore_Sun_A-1

1953_03_22_Chicago_Tribune_p22

1953_03_22_New_York_Times_p5

1953_04_26_Hartford_Courant_pB-10

1953_04_30_Los_Angeles_Times_p23

1953_07_31_Los_Angeles_Times_p21

1953_07_31_Washington_Post_p8

1953_08_04_Hartford_Courant_p33

1953_08_21_Hartford_Courant_p2

1953_08_21_Pittsburgh_Press_p7

1953_08_26_Hartford_Courant_p1-A

1953_08_29_New_York_Times_p2

1953_09_14_Life_p63

1953_09_15_Chicago_Tribune_pB-7

1953_09_15_Washington_Post_p13

1953_09_16_Chicago_Tribune_pA-9

1953_09_17_Hartford_Courant_p3

1953_09_22_Hartford_Courant_p1

1953_10_13_Chicago_Tribune_p3

1953_10_13_Los_Angeles_Times_p8

1953_10_20_Chicago_Tribune_p5

1953_10_21_New_York_Times_p10

1953_10_22_Huntingdon_Daily_News_p17

1953_10_26_New_York_Times_p7

1953_10_28_Washington_Post_p11

1953_11_29_Independent_Press_Telegram_p131

Hee-Haw (1954)

1953_01_23_Standard-Sentinel_p4

1953_03_10_Indianapolis_News_p2

1954_11_30_Central_New_Jersey_Home_News_p1

1954_11_30_The_Town_Talk_p13

1954_12_06_Central_New_Jersey_Home_News_p20

1954_12_07_Madisonville_Messenger_p1

1954_12_08_Los_Angeles_Times_pII-8

1954_12_22_Lubbock_Evening_Journal_p7

1955_01_02_Pensacola_News_Journal_p7-D

1955_01_03_Corsicana_Daily_Sun_p3

1955_01_30_Denton_Record-Chronicle_p5

1955_01_30_Lubbock_Avalanche-Journal_pII-5

1955_02_13_Tampa_Tribune_p10-C

1955_02_15_Miami_Daily_News-Record_p3

1955_02_20_Louisville_Courier-Journal_p5-7

1955_02_20_Louisville_Courier-Journal_p5-7-a

1955_02_24_Allentown_Morning-Call_p23

1955_02_27_Shreveport_Times_p6-D

1955_03_11_Corpus_Christi_Caller-Times_p33

1955_03_13_Central_New_Jersey_Home_News_p2

1955_03_20_Daily_Oklahoman_pA-13

1955_03_23_Idaho_State_Journal_p1

1955_04_03_Arizona_Republic-Arizona_Days_and_Ways_p4

1955_04_10_El_Paso_Times_p26

1955_04_24_Waterloo_Courier_p32

1955_05_03_Battle_Creek_Enquirer_p1

1955_05_05_Bridgeport_Post_p69

1955_05_06_Hartford_Courant_p38-A

1955_05_07_Biloxi_Daily_Herald_p8

1955_05_08_Hartford_Courant_pA-5

1955_05_08_Syracuse_Post-Standard_p34

1955_05_10_Hartford_Courant_p2

1955_05_10_Lima_News_p21

1955_05_10_Washington_Post_and_Times_Herald_p10

1955_05_11_Oakland_Tribune_p31

1955_05_12_Traverse_City_Record_Eagle_p3

1955_12_12_Atlanta_Constitution_p3

1956_04_01_Arizona_Daily_Star_pD-10

1956_04_11_Arizona_Republic_p4

1956_08_26_Arizona_Daily_Star_p6

1956_08_30_Arizona_Republic_p28

1959_12_25_Clarion-Ledger_p6

1963_01_09_Orangeburg_Times_and_Democrat_p3

1966_02_05_Troy_Times_Record_p3

The Shoe Bandit (1956)

1953_08_08_Bakersfield_Californian_p14

1956_09_20_Coronado_Eagle_and_Journal_p1

1956_09_27_Coronado_Eagle_and_Journal_p1

1956_10_04_Coronado_Eagle_and_Journal_p1

1956_10_11_Coronado_Eagle_and_Journal_p1

1956_11_01_Coronado_Eagle_and_Journal_p1

1956_11_22_Coronado_Eagle_and_Journal_p1

1956_12_13_Coronado_Eagle_and_Journal_p1

1957_01_10_Coronado_Eagle_and_Journal_p1

1957_02_20_Santa_Maria_Times_p1

1957_02_28_Coronado_Eagle_and_Journal_p1

1957_03_12_San_Bernardino_County_Sun_p18

1957_03_13_San_Bernardino_County_Sun_p1

1957_03_21_Coronado_Eagle_and_Journal_p1

1957_04_11_Coronado_Eagle_and_Journal_p1

1957_08_18_Independent_Star-News_p3

1958_05_01_Coronado_Eagle_and_Journal_p7

1958_05_09_Atlanta_Constitution_p15

1958_05_09_Daily_Independent_Journal_p9

1958_05_09_Kansas_City_Times_p1.JPG

1958_05_09_Los_Angeles_Times_pB6

1958_05_09_Santa_Fe_New_Mexican_p9

1958_05_10_Amarillo_Daily_News_p4

1958_05_14_Springfield_Leader_and_Press_p2

1958_05_15_Coronado_Eagle_and_Journal_p12

1958_05_16_Brownsville_Herald_p1

1958_06_10_Los_Angeles_Times_pA7

1958_06_11_Arizona_Republic_p1

1958_06_11_Valley_Morning_Star_p5

1958_07_18_Kansas_City_Times_p6

1958_08_19_ Los_Angeles_Times_p25

1958_08_19_Santa_Maria_Times_p6

1958_08_19_Valley_Morning_Star_p5

1958_11_06_Brownwood_Bulletin_p1

1959_01_24_Redlands_Daily_Facts_p1

1960_03_17_Albuquerque_Journal_p7

1969_08_23_Oakland_Tribune_p26

Two Weeks on Venus (1956)

1917_07_19_Chattanooga_Times_p7

1917_07_22_Chattanooga_Sunday_Times_p7

1917_07_23_State_Journal_p7

1957_03_26_Billings_Gazette_p7

1957_03_26_Corpus_Christi_Times_p4

1957_03_28_Florence_Morning_News_p20

1957_03_29_Van_Wert_Times_Bulletin_p8

1957_04_06_Steuben_Advocate_p1

1957_04_10_Washington_Post_pC-7

1957_04_17_Daily_Journal_p4

1957_05_17_Washington_Post_pD-9

1957_05_18_Cumberland_News_p2

1957_05_18_Morning_Herald_p3

1957_10_04_Lawrence_Journal_World_p2

1957_12_14_Washington_Post_pB-3

1961_05_21_Los_Angeles_Times_pB-8

The Flying Bandits (1957)

1957_10_24_Tampa_Times_p1

1957_10_25_Tampa_Daily_Times_p1

1957_10_25_Tampa_Morning_Tribune_p1

1957_10_26_Tampa_Bay_Times_p8

1957_10_26_Tampa_Daily_Times_p2

1957_10_26_Tampa_Tribune_p1

1957_10_27_Tampa_Bay_Times_p8

1957_10_27_Tampa_Sunday_Tribune_p1

1957_10_28_Tampa_Daily_Times_p1

1957_10_28_Tampa_Times_p2

1957_10_28_Tampa_Tribune_p5

1957_10_29_Tampa_Times_p1

1957_10_29_Tampa_Tribune_p11

1957_10_30_Tampa_Times_p2

1957_10_30_Tampa_Tribune_p6

1957_11_04_Tampa_Times_p1

1957_11_05_Tampa_Bay_Times_p26

1957_11_05_Tampa_Morning_Tribune_p3

1957_11_25_Tampa_Daily_Times_p1

1957_11_26_Tampa_Bay_Times_p1

1957_11_26_Tampa_Tribune_p1

1957_11_27_Tampa_Times_p2

1957_11_28_Tampa_Tribune_p4

1958_06_11_Roseburg_News-Review_p1

1961_08_02_Tampa_Times_p3

1971_10_24_Tampa_Bay_Times_p1

1971_10_25_Tampa_Tribune_p13-A

It Doesn't Always Pay to Be a Hero (1957)

1957_04_14_Salina_Journal_p2

Kidnapper Rides on Car Hood in Nightgown (1964)

1964_08_18_Greenville_News_p3

1964_08_18_Hartford_Courant_p21-E

1964_10_06_Burlington_Daily_News_p20

1965_05_11_Kannapolis_Daily_Independent_p1

Love for Lease (1965)

1965_12_12_Arizona_Daily_Star_p36

1965_12_21_Arizona_Daily_Star_p21

1965_12_28_Tucson_Daily_Citizen_p4

1966_08_05_Tucson_Daily_Citizen_p25

1966_08_06_Arizona_Daily_Star_p4

1966_10_11_New_York_Daily_News_p4

1966_10_30_New_York_Daily_News_p9

1966_11_09_New_York_Daily_News_p48-S

1967_02_22_New_York_Daily_News_p3

1967_02_23_New_York_Daily_News_p4

1967_02_24_New_York_Daily_News_p7

1967_02_25_New_York_Daily_News_pC-8

1967_02_26_New_York_Daily_News_p5

1967_02_28_Arizona_Republic_p25

1967_02_28_New_York_Daily_News_p4-C

Smokin' Bananas (1967)

1967_03_05_Santa_Rosa_Press_Democrat_p8-A

1967_03_15_Detroit_Free_Press_p4

1967_03_17_San_Francisco_Examiner_p35

1967_03_19_Chula_Vista_Star-News_p16

1967_03_27_Long_Beach_Independent_p3

1967_03_31_Salt_Lake_Tribune_p6

1967_04_03_Allentown_Morning_Call_p2

1967_04_04_Chicago_Tribune_pA-8

1967_04_05_Boston_Globe_p22

1967_04_05_New_York_Times_p49

1967_04_06_Arizona_Republic_p27

1967_04_07_San_Bernardino_County_Sun_p19

1967_04_13_Hartford_Courant_p9

1967_04_13_Washington_Post_pE3

1967_04_17_Baltimore_Evening_Sun_p21

1967_04_17_Nashua_Telegraph_p8

1967_04_19_Congressional_Record_p10084

1967_04_19_Los_Angeles_Times_p3

1967_04_25_Camden_Courier-Post_p15

1967_05_25_The_Tennessean_p9

1967_06_11_Los_Angeles_Times_pL-41

1967_09_08_New_Castle_News_p4

1967_11_12_New_York_Times_p70

1967_12_10_Nashville_Tennessean_p11-G

1969_04_06_Los_Angeles_Times_pB-1

The Crayola Caper (1973)

1973_10_10_Philadelphia_Inquirer_p4

1973_10_12_Washington_Post_pD-19

1974_11_13_Utica_Daily_Press_p33

1974_11_14_Lebanon_Daily_News_p54

1974_11_16_Citizen_Advertiser_p2

1974_11_16_Daily_Press_p2

1974_11_16_Middletown_Times_Herald_Record_p7

1975_01_11_Tyrone_Daily_Herald_p4

1975_01_11_Utica_Daily_Press_p3

ACKNOWLEDGEMENTS

It is on the shoulders of long-forgotten reporters and authors that this book has been built. I owe the greatest of thanks to those who worked hard reporting these stories when they first made headlines decades ago.

Thanks to M.H.A. for all of the hard work she's done researching her great-grandfather, Harold Jesse Berney.

The story on the Salem Trade School football team would have been incomplete without the incredible assistance of John Murphy. His dad's diary offered insight that could never be obtained from newspaper archives.

Thanks to my friend Jamie Keenan for penning the "About the Author" section in this book, and for starting me down this winding road of writing and podcasting.

Lastly, special thanks to my friend Barbara Roosevelt who gave up much of her retirement to help me edit this book.

ABOUT THE AUTHOR

Steve Silverman is a veteran science teacher, business owner, patent holder, podcaster, talented storyteller, and all-around great guy. Early on in his career, he began collecting unusual stories in order to grab his students' attention. His quirky stories, fun labs, and annual "set my tie on fire" day led his students to start an annual Steve Silverman Day, which is celebrated every May at Chatham High School in Chatham, New York.

In 1994, Steve started his Useless Information platform, one of the first 25,000 sites on what was then the new World Wide Web. The website's popularity exploded when it was chosen by Yahoo! as its Pick of the Week in July of 1997. This led Steve to share more of his stories in book form. *Einstein's Refrigerator* was published in 2001, and was quickly followed by *Lindbergh's Artificial Heart* in 2003. He began entertaining and informing people with his *Useless Information* podcast in 2008, and is still entertaining listeners today.

A lifelong animal lover, Steve and his brother also owned an online pet business that specialized in hermit crab supplies. In his spare time, Steve enjoys remodeling his one-hundred-year-old home, finding interesting antiques, and biking with his wife Mary Jane.

Podcast: *Useless Information Podcast*
Website: www.uselessinformation.org
Email: steve@uselessinformation.org
Facebook: uselessinformationpodcast
Twitter: @UselessInfoCast

Mango Publishing, established in 2014, publishes an eclectic list of books by diverse authors—both new and established voices—on topics ranging from business, personal growth, women's empowerment, LGBTQ studies, health, and spirituality to history, popular culture, time management, decluttering, lifestyle, mental wellness, aging, and sustainable living.

We were recently named 2020's #1 fastest growing independent publisher by *Publishers Weekly*. Our success is driven by our main goal, which is to publish high quality books that will entertain readers as well as make a positive difference in their lives.

Our readers are our most important resource; we value your input, suggestions, and ideas. We'd love to hear from you—after all, we are publishing books for you!

Please stay in touch with us and follow us at:

Facebook: Mango Publishing
Twitter: @MangoPublishing
Instagram: @MangoPublishing
LinkedIn: Mango Publishing
Pinterest: Mango Publishing

Sign up for our newsletter at www.mango.bz and receive a free book!

Join us on Mango's journey to reinvent publishing, one book at a time.